The Tribulations of Sophia

Other Books of Interest from St. Augustine's Press

Étienne Gilson, *Theology and the Cartesian Doctrine of Freedom*

Josef Seifert, *Christian Philosophy and Free Will*

Stanley Rosen, *Metaphysics in Ordinary Language*

Stanley Rosen, *Platonic Productions: Theme and Variations*

Stanley Rosen, *The Limits of Analysis*

Nalin Ranasinghe (Editor),
Logos and Eros: Essays Honoring Stanley Rosen

Peter Kreeft, *Socrates' Children: The 100 Greatest Philosophers*

Peter Kreeft, *Ethics for Beginners: 52 Big Ideas from 32 Great Minds*

John von Heyking, *Comprehensive Judgment and Absolute Selflessness:
Winston Churchill on Politics as Friendship*

Joseph Bottum, *The Decline of the Novel*

Barry Cooper, *Consciousness and Politics:
From Analysis to Meditation in the Late Work of Eric Voegelin*

D. Q. McInerny, *Being Ethical*

Roger Scruton, *The Politics of Culture and Other Essays*

Roger Scruton, *The Meaning of Conservatism*

Roger Scruton, *An Intelligent Person's Guide to Modern Culture*

James V. Schall, *On the Principles of Taxing Beer*

Edward Feser, *Neo-Scholastic Essays*

Edward Feser, *The Last Superstition*

Winston Churchill, *The River War*

Gene Fendt, *Camus' Plague: Myth for Our World*

Fulvio Di Blasi, *From Aristotle to Thomas Aquinas: Natural Law, Practical
Knowledge, and the Person*

Alexandre Kojève, *The Idea of Determinism*

Alexandre Kojève, *The Concept, Time, and Discourse*

The Tribulations of Sophia
ÉTIENNE GILSON
Translated by James G. Colbert

ST. AUGUSTINE'S PRESS
South Bend, Indiana

Manufactured in the United States of America.

1 2 3 4 5 6   26 25 24 23 22 21

Library of Congress Control Number: 2021942954

∞ The paper used in this publication meets the minimum
requirements of the American National Standard for Information Sciences –
Permanence of Paper for Printed Materials, ANSI Z39.48-1984.

St. Augustine's Press
www.staugustine.net

Table of Contents

Preface

The birth of this little book was neither anticipated nor desired. Therein lies the explanation of its varied content. Professor Irma Antonetto, who is the guiding spirit of an association that sponsors lectures in French at Turin, had been inviting me for several years to visit four Italian cities: Turin, Milan, Rome, and Naples. The seventh centenary of Dante's birth gave me the duty of visiting Florence in April 1965 and the occasion to accept Dr. Antonetto's invitation. Dr. Antonetto's ingenuity found a way to combine the two projects, and I had to submit a list of possible topics for the promised lectures. Reviewing the list, the idea occurred to me to add, just in case, a talk on St. Thomas Aquinas and the contemporary situation of Thomism. To my great surprise, three of the four cities declared themselves in favor of this topic. So I accepted, but since I had no desire to give the same lecture three times in a row, I prepared three different lectures under the same title. These are the "Three Lectures on Thomism and Its Contemporary Situation," which constitute the bulk of this work.

Word, however muted, reached the Roman Curia, and Bishop Dino Staffa, secretary of the Sacred Congregation of Seminaries and Universities at the time, expressed the desire to publish the lectures in the Vatican journal *Seminarium*. I gratefully accepted the honor, and the text of the three lectures appeared in number four of 1965. Nowadays it is hard to speak of any theological subject without encountering Teilhard de Chardin. If you seek to avoid him, people trip you with him. Accordingly, I said a few words about him in the third lecture. Bishop Staffa requested me to take up the question in greater detail, which I did unenthusiastically in what constitutes chapter four of the present work, "The Teilhard de Chardin Case."

I say that I did it unenthusiastically because nothing is less gratifying, more tedious, and ultimately more sterile than negative discussion. We tend to understand badly a way of thinking with which we are in complete disagreement. I must confess, furthermore, that, as much as I feel ready to criticize a firm, articulate, coherent, and fully defined way of thinking, it is painful for me to take issue with as elusive an opus as Teilhard's. The confusion there is such that you cannot discuss it without soon feeling lost and no longer knowing what you are talking about. Descartes complained about certain scholastics that their mode of philosophizing made them invulnerable to attack, because, he said, the obscurity of their principles allowed them "to speak of everything as boldly as if they knew it and to maintain everything they said about it against the most subtle and skilled opponents without there being a way to convince them." In this, he adds, "They seem like a blind person to me, who in order to fight on equal terms against someone who is sighted, would have made him come to the depths of some dark cave." Teilhard does not make one descend into a cave. On the contrary, he is like the pilot of a plane who never touches the ground and finds himself in the clouds as in his natural element. Poets have the right and perhaps the duty to be that way, but I confess that dealing with prose, I like a writer who lets me know exactly the meaning of what he says. Quite recently, I still believed that I could succeed with Teilhard here, by putting his exegetes on notice that they were to justify this or that affirmation that seemed free from all ambiguity. But I now know that nothing is gained by adopting this method, because to the objection that Teilhard has said something, his friends respond good naturedly that he said the opposite many times. And it is often true, but that does not facilitate philosophical conversation. I remember that Albert Bazaillas, in the course of his thesis defense, felt a little too pressed by the dialectic of the professor who presided and ended by exclaiming, "I demand the right to be obscure." To this Victor Brochard simply responded, "You have it, but do not abuse it."

Rereading what I agreed to write then, I do not see that I have wronged the thought or the memory of the distinguished Jesuit. I recall the time when the Collège de France was preparing to create a chair for him. The affair was practically settled, and we all would have voted for him. At the last minute, our Administrator informed us that Father Teilhard's superiors did not authorize him to present his candidacy. With perfect fidelity to his religious profession, he bowed to their decision, an occurrence which often makes me wonder at how everything connected to this man is bathed in mystery. If his act of obedience was really heroic, the inflexible rigidity of his superiors that day protected the Collège de France from a formidable danger. At that period of his life, Father Teilhard's mind dwelled in the noosphere more readily than in the Pliocene. Now the noosphere is no more a scientific concept then the Empyrean. It is a new *caelum theologicum*.

However that may be, this fourth chapter is not a lecture delivered in Italy. It is an essay written to respond to a request by Bishop Dino Staffa to have my opinion on Fr. Teilhard's thought, taken in itself and not obliquely, as a possible substitute for that of St. Thomas Aquinas.

Chapter five has yet a different origin. As will be seen, it responds to a book by Roger Garaudy, *De l'anthème au Concile*. It has nothing to do with the Italian lectures, and it was I who proposed it to Bishop Staffa, requesting that he please accept it for *Seminarium*. The offer was graciously received. I composed the piece thinking that this bit of Communist propaganda might cause harm that it was urgent to prevent, but Roman prudence seems not to have judged that there was danger in delay. *Seminarium* published "The Difficult Dialogue" in number 4 of 1966. Meanwhile Dino Staffa, who had presided over *Seminarium* and greatly contributed to its orientation, had been promoted to other posts in the Papal Curia. Furthermore, the article was only published under the section of *Discussioni*. The author could not complain that the new editors attributed more importance to his opinions than they have.

Chapter six, an entirely new composition, is also new in the sentiment that motivated it. I saw and knew nothing of the Second Vatican Council but its consequences. I confess that so far, they have neither surprised nor disturbed me. Changes occurred, but the original intention of Pope John XXIII was that they should. The faithful have not been involved in these changes at all. They have only undergone them, if not always without protest, at least without revolt. Their docility is the more remarkable given that the reform that affects them directly concerns the liturgy, that is, the language in which they address God. No one consulted them. They did not even know who originated the reforms. Their questions continue unanswered. In short, the flock of faithful has never deserved its name more. The reason why there will still be no revolt is that the Christian people, at least in France, has ceased to take these things as matters of life and death. The elderly will continue to pray in their fashion. The young will find quite natural what they have been taught. The *Magnificat*, badly transformed into a drinking song, with verses and chorus, will fully satisfy people whose poetic and musical demands are modest. There is nothing about which we ought to be disturbed.

The reason I wrote this last chapter is different. Over many years I have developed the routine of a three-month stay in the United Sates and Canada. Recently, the stay confronted me with a new situation. Returning from the U.S. Georges Duhamel once summed up his impressions in a book entitled *Scenes from Future Life* (*Scènes de la vie future*). He intended to make us aware that America's today could well become our own tomorrow. The book's provincialism and haste to disapprove of all foreigners who change its customs annoyed me, but some of its predictions have come to pass. We are becoming Americanized before our very eyes, and I wonder whether what is happening over there today is not in danger of happening one day among us. Perhaps I might have done better not to share my concerns, but I believed I ought to discretely inform French Catholics about what is in store for them if they persist unreflectively in following paths whose only merit is their novelty. When I am tempted to worry, I console myself with the thought that when one has no possibility of taking action, one is thereby free from all responsibility.

Let us render to the Countess of Ségur, née Rostopchine, what is due her. She published *The Misfortunes of Sophia* (*Les malheurs de Sophie*) in 1864 and the title unquestionably belongs to her. Her Sophia was a supposedly real little girl whose misfortunes were not wholly undeserved.[1] What Paul Claudel brought to the stage, by contrast, was clearly symbolic and scriptural: the formidable Judith, the touching Esther, and other personalities from Sacred History in whom Sophia takes flesh are those figures that, according to Saint Hilaire, all lead back to Christ. The new Sophia, whose misfortunes I lament, is not a little girl or an allegory but none other than wisdom, *sophia*, *sapientia*. She is the doctrine that St. Thomas called supreme wisdom among all human wisdoms and not only in a particular

---

1   [Translator: for North Americans unfamiliar with the story, Sophie is a young aristocratic girl, a nineteenth-century Dennis the Menace who leaves a trail of dead pets in her wake. The Countess's tale is not to be confused with the last work of Paul Claudel, *Les aventures de Sophie*, 1937.]

genus but absolutely. *Maxime sapientia est inter omnes sapientias humanas, non quidem in aliquo genere tantum sed simpliciter.*

It has become difficult for the simple believer to know what is taught by this wisdom that takes its principles from God's own knowledge. Popes tell him and have repeated the message untiringly for at least five centuries, but priests do not always concur with Popes on that, and therefore they do not agree among themselves. If a simple member of the faithful says he agrees with the Popes, theologians often frown upon him.

Theology is a wisdom that is the sister of Mary. She is far from despising action, but she first must pass through contemplation. Vatican II never claimed to abolish Vatican I. On the contrary, it proposed to crown it and bring it to completion by making it bear fruit. Some conclude from this that pastoral theology will replace dogmatic theology. By losing sight of the latter, Wisdom fragments into different wisdoms, without a compass to counsel us about divergent paths. Disorder invades Christianity today. It will only cease when dogmatic theology regains its natural primacy over practice. We ought to be able to regret that it has ever been threatened with losing that primacy. There is no trace of rebellion in this complaint. Those who so often lament that the Church lost a hearing among almost a whole social class still ought to understand that alienating herself from another social class is not a good way to regain that hearing.

April 30, 1967

Part I:
Three Lessons on Thomism and Its Current Situation

I

An Untimely Theologian

Perhaps a few words of explanation about the title of this talk might be useful. My personal experience gave me the inspiration for the topic, but I think that I share it with most of those who, were they to encounter St. Thomas in the next life, would be disposed to greet him with the words that Dante addresses to Virgil at the beginning of the *Divine Comedy*:

> *Tu se' lo mio maestro e'l mio autore.*

Nothing is easier to say or more satisfying. At first glance nothing poses fewer problems. Those who speak this way are, like me, most often Christians and even Catholics. They know themselves to be members of a Church that has chosen Thomas Aquinas as its Common Doctor. Their preferred personal Doctor turns out to be at the same time the one the Church assigns as the Doctor of all its faithful. A more satisfying situation could not be imagined, and truly it is for the best. Almost a century ago, Pope Leo XIII mandated that the saint's doctrine be taught in all Catholic schools and that no Christian teacher should commit the imprudence of deviating from his principles in any way. Finally, in an extraordinary and, in a way, unique decision, canon law made the doctrinal decision into a legal obligation in some sense. Consequently, a Catholic teacher has the duty to teach Thomist doctrine in virtue of canon law. He is obligated to be a Thomist, so to speak, "in the name of the law."

These official mandates hardly affect those who are Thomists by personal preference. Not only do they fail to understand that one might be obligated to do what they are happy to do, or obligated to profess a doctrine whose study is their delight, but they loathe hearing that they are Thomists because the Pope requires them to be so. It must be confessed that the situation at first sight is a little ridiculous. It seems that there are some countries today where an official philosophy holds sway in government, the civil service, and the schools. I do not know what the situation is in Russia today, but I know well that when I went there in 1919, the local St. Thomas was named Karl Marx. In philosophical questions and in some others, one was a Marxist, and one could not be anything else. That seemed a little boring in the long run. When the answers to every question are known ahead of time, the conversation has no surprises. Only carelessness can be counted on to produce them. I recall one day that, passing through the city of Kharkov by train and viewing what could be seen from the station, I remarked unthinkingly to my neighbor, an amiable People's Commissar with whom I was chatting, "This is a very big city." "Yes," he replied, "and above all, it is a modern city: few churches, but many factory chimneys." Impelled by an evil spirit, I replied in turn, "That is true, but I see no smoke." "Ah," answered my Commissar, "that is because it is Sunday." I thought he was straying from the Party line here. Why would Marxist chimneys emit less smoke on Sunday than other days? But it seemed more courteous not to put him on the spot, from which he would have extracted himself anyway, because he had a Marxist answer for everything. I only remember that after five or six days of journey and indoctrination, I felt despondent about the prospect of any further conversation.

Sometimes I am afraid to think that certain people depict the situation of Thomism within the Church as analogous with that of Marxism in Communist countries. If matters stood this way, it would be dreadful, and at least for me intolerable, but are they? Is Thomism something like a "Party line" within the Church?

When I look around me, I first of all see a multitude of Catholics, often among the best, who dispense with any philosophy and even with any theology, if by theology we understand a scholarly reflection about Christian faith. The Church cannot dispense with theology nor a Christian with religious faith and dogmas, but a Christian can gain salvation without being a theologian and even more without being a philosopher. Far and away the greater number of them are neither Thomists nor anything else. They are Christians, which is the essential thing, and it suffices.

Looking toward contemporary theologians and philosophers, I would say that what I see first is the immense and noble multitude of Augustinians.

Like St. Augustine, they approach God by a kind of speculative deepening of their Christian religious life. Their proofs of the existence of God are a meditation upon the truth and light of the Word in which we know that existence. Love, charity, is more important to them than knowledge, and Thomistic intellectualism repels them with a kind of dryness that chills them. If I were asked what theology most impacted the development of the great modern philosophies, I would reply unhesitatingly St. Augustine's. In France, Descartes, Pascal, Malebranche, Maine de Biran, Maurice Blondel, all bear more or less deeply the stamp of Augustinianism. In Italy, Sigismond Gerdil, Rosmini-Serbati, and Gioberti have developed Malebranche's Augustinianism with originality and often depth. And it would be easy to cite countries where, to judge by the great modern doctrines they have produced, the impact of Thomism has been meager. England and Germany, the promised land of metaphysical speculation, are hardly inspired by the teaching of St. Thomas Aquinas. Outside the theological schools properly speaking, which are a special case, Thomism hardly has children. In Spain, the doctrine of Balmes is rather a variety of common sense philosophy.

What do we see in the schools of Christian philosophy and theology? If I am not mistaken, the largest order is that of the least philosophical founder, St. Francis of Assisi, who was not much more of a theologian than a philosopher. Without having conducted special research on the subject, I do not have the impression that the Franciscan order or the Franciscan family are particularly intense focal points for Thomistic theology. There are certainly religious orders which declare themselves for St. Thomas Aquinas, but in such cases, we must always ask with which St. Thomas we are dealing. Perhaps it may be St. Thomas revised and corrected by Francisco Suárez, who has been much taught in the schools of the Society of Jesus and perhaps is still taught there. Fr. Pedro Descoqs, S.J., whom I knew well, would have felt his religious vocation waiver if someone had wished to make him accept certain fundamental Thomistic theses like the composition of essence and existence in finite beings.

I am well aware that there is the Order of St. Dominic, where one is a Thomist by the very fact that one is a Dominican, but which St. Thomas is it whose doctrine is followed there? Perhaps it is the St. Thomas of the *Summa Theologiae*, and indeed it often is, but will we follow the *Summa* itself or will we not rather follow the commentary by Cajetan that accompanies it? For it is not the same thing, and one cannot teach both doctrines at the same time. Naturally, there are other Thomisms to choose from, among which we can exercise a kind of option, no doubt rational, but free. I am well aware that there is a historical vision, based moreover on the highest authorities of the Church, according to which one indivisible Thomist school has endured from St. Thomas to our times. I personally think after many years of study, that this doctrinal unity of the Thomist school has been greatly exaggerated. We can see that sometimes quite deeply variant Thomisms had been established immediately after the death of the master, whom everyone respected and admired. An example that I think typical will perhaps dispense me from long considerations. At the beginning of the fourteenth century, the Dominican Hervaeus Natalis, Master General of the Order of Preachers took care that St. Thomas's doctrine should be considered that of the whole order. For him, to be a Dominican was to be a Thomist. However, in his own writings, he refused to accept that finite beings are really composed of their essence and of a distinct act that would be their act of being. To reject the composition of essence and existence in the finite being, which innumerable philosophers and theologians have done, is to reject what is most personally Thomistic in St. Thomas's theology. However, not only Hervaeus Natalis but also Cajetan himself, whose commentary embellishes the text of the *Summa Theologiae* in the Leonine edition, refused to accept it. I have personally known famous masters within St. Dominic's order, who set forth the Thomistic doctrine and its fundamental theses without making the slightest allusion to the thesis of the composition of essence and existence. I do not blame them. Very jealous of my own freedom, I greatly respect that of others. But we are not dealing with philosophical or theological opinion. We are dealing with a historical fact. We ask where, in fact, the authentic doctrine of St. Thomas Aquinas has been taught. I think I can insist that it is not enough for a master to call himself a Thomist, or even to think he is, for us to be sure that we are dealing with a faithful disciple of St. Thomas. I would go further. On the strength of my personal experience, I could cite two or three important theses of St. Thomas that I have never brought up as his, quoting them in his own words, theses I did not even say were *true* but only that they were *Thomistic*, without before long having on my hands illustrious theologians, Dominicans or not, but all Thomists, writing in Thomistic journals to accuse me of bordering on heresy.

To avoid being accused of arbitrariness, let me offer you two of St. Thomas's positions that it is difficult to present without raising a protest in certain minds, zealous for orthodoxy. The first, about which there have been endless controversies, is that "every intellect naturally desires to see the divine substance." Merely venture this proposition in good theological company, and you will see what happens to you. I do not say, "Venture this proposition as true," but simply as St. Thomas's genuine thought. Yet he certainly said: *Omnis intellectus naturaliter desiderat divinae substantiae visionem* (*Summa Contra Gentiles* III, 57, 4). Personally I admit that others may reject this proposition. I do not believe in philosophical authority. I have no theological authority. As I have said, I am particularly careful of the freedom of everybody. I only say this: maintain as much as you like that the understanding does not *naturally* desire to see God. Even hold that it is dangerous for faith to teach this thesis, if that is your opinion. But do not maintain that it is possible to deny it and still be a Thomist. St. Thomas's whole thought is at stake here, and no authority in the world can cause him not to have written that sentence printed in the Leonine edition of his complete works. There is nothing to do about that.

Here is a second example, which succeeds inevitably. In a meeting of Catholic philosophers and theologians, that is to say Thomists, say that what God is remains completely unknown to us. You may rest assured that you will immediately hear yourself accused of agnosticism. Matters will go no better if, seeking a different expression, you say, "I know well that God's existence is known to us, I only say that *what God is* is unknown to us and even entirely unknown." It will be repeated that you are an agnostic, and you will never cleanse yourself of the accusation. So be it, but what is impossible for me to deny is that such is St. Thomas Aquinas's doctrine. We know what God is not, says the Common Doctor in the Leonine edition of *Summa Contra Gentiles*, III, 49, 9: "quid vero sit *penitus* manet ignotum." He does not say, "badly known," "almost unknown," but completely unknown. It is impossible to know something less than what is *penitus incognitum*. *Omnino ignotum* St. Thomas says elsewhere (*In Librum De Causis*, prop. 6), and again: *Sicut eius substantia est ignota, ita est esse* (*Quaestiones Disputatae de Potentia*, 7, 2, ad 1ᵐ). Is this true or not? My personal opinion on the matter has no importance. But whether St. Thomas said it or not is another matter, and on that score, I can guarantee that no doubt is possible.

He said it and said it again, and if anyone claims to be a Thomist while teaching that we know what God is, I will not deny that this is possible in order to avoid troubling him. I will content myself with affirming that I do not understand what he says.

It is odd, however, and the simple narration of these two facts — many others could be mentioned — is enough to make what I want to say intelligible by suggesting that in great measure the Common Doctor's universal teaching authority is a matter of principle much more than a reality with no exceptions. The exceptions are real, numerous, and active. If I did not desire above all to avoid emotionalizing the discussion, I could make it clear that several are aggressive. I have never reproached anyone for not being a Thomist, but I have often been reproached for being one. I have even been reproached for wanting to re-ignite the pyres of the Inquisition, as if there could still be an issue of pyres when modern progress has invented the electric chair! A philosopher is not surprised at much. I simply observe that our relation to St. Thomas is not as simple as might be imagined. He who strives to rediscover the Common Doctor's true mind — an endeavor that is long, difficult, and full of risks — finds himself at the end of his effort belonging to a minority within a minority.

If he could only hope that general approval of his effort would be guaranteed within that minority! That would seem a minimum, because, in the last analysis, as his Holiness Pope Paul VI recently recalled again to the Dominicans of the United States, when St. Thomas is the issue, the matter is to defend something greater than he: *maius aliquid in Sancto Thoma quam Sanctus Thomas suscipitur et defenditur.* I do not believe I am mistaken in thinking that a sort of anti-Thomist offensive is being prepared in quarters where nothing would have invited us to foresee it. Since personal experience is naturally what impresses us the most, let me mention a very recent one, which, you will understand, particularly interests me.

Some years ago an association was established in Quebec to promote the Leonine edition of the works of St. Thomas Aquinas. Three or four years later, this society asked me to be its honorary president, which seemed hard to refuse. At the end of 1963 or 1964, the society invited me to give a lecture to interest the general public in the undertaking and gain support for it. The honorary president of the society could not shy away. The date of the lecture was set several months in advance for Monday, November 16 at 8 p.m. On the morning

14

of November 16 a Dominican father, who is a friend, handed me a local newspaper of that date, with a bold headline announcing: "The Church should not give exclusive importance to St. Thomas." I would like to pretend to believe that it was mere coincidence, but it summoned me to reflection. By way of welcome to a visitor who had just crossed the Atlantic to cooperate in an eminently ecclesiastical activity, it was rather a wet blanket. But it is necessary to know how to take advantage of everything, and the incident at least provided me with a typical example of a reaction even in high places that would tend nowadays to moderate our allegiance to St. Thomas Aquinas.

Naturally, there is a reason for all these attitudes, and it is appropriate to examine the main ones.

What struck me first is that it is hard to know what people are talking about. We are told that the Church ought not to rest its teaching "upon one single doctor." To consider a thirteenth-century philosopher like St. Thomas as the Catholic Church's "official" theologian troubles some people. What are these reproaches about? If the issue is about St. Thomas *philosopher*, one does not see how he could be any Church's *theologian*, official or not. And the first clarification is required here. As such, the Church does not teach any philosophy, Thomist, Scotist, Suarezian, or other. Philosophy as such belongs to the temporal order. Like physics, biology, or any other natural science, philosophy is "of this world." The Church has no particular responsibility in this regard. When Aristotle elaborated his philosophy, the Christian church did not yet exist, and no Greek thinker could foresee its advent. Aristotelianism did not become a religious revelation after the thirteenth century A.D., and just as one could be saved during the first twelve centuries of the Christian era, the gospel without Aristotle still ought to suffice today for the salvation of humanity. The same thing is true for any philosopher whatsoever and any philosophical doctrine at all, even St. Thomas Aquinas himself and his doctrine. If it is true that St. Thomas became the "official" doctor of the Church, that cannot be Thomas philosopher but only Thomas theologian.

But then, what will we say about all this noise about philosophy in general and St. Thomas's philosophy in particular? I will try to give as simple as possible an answer to this question, whose elements, however, are extremely complicated, so much so that in particular detail their complication becomes infinite.

The principle of the answer is easily grasped: it is not the Church that concerns itself with the teaching of the philosophers; it is the philosophers who continually involve themselves in the teaching of the Church. I could take examples from what is happening in our time, but I would appear to engage in controversy. So allow me to direct myself to the past and to its history. Since our personal feelings are not at stake perhaps we will see things more clearly.

Reading the Index of Forbidden Books is at the same time discouraging and quite instructive. Discouraging because the fruitlessness of these condemnations becomes obvious, but instructive in many ways. Primarily, because of all the philosophies once condemned, there is perhaps not a single one held to be true by anyone at all today. Yet, in their times, the partisans of these philosophies judged it indispensable to renounce traditional theology in order to proceed to an *aggiornamento*. In the case of René Descartes, I do not see why any of his works should be on the Index, but I see quite well why Rome considered the doctrine suspect. Besides being a great mathematician and a very original philosopher, there was an apostle and a reformer in Descartes. He wished to reform the education of secondary schools, all of which were religious at the time. To replace Aristotle's doctrine he wrote his *Principles of Philosophy* conceived as a manual for school use. He even intended to furnish a definition of the miracle of transubstantiation, based on his own notion of matter as identical to extension without substance or accidents. No doubt, you see nothing wrong there. Nor do I. No philosophy has as its function to explain miracles, no more Descartes's philosophy than Aristotle's. A theologian can only define miracles. The point I am considering is different. It is that twenty years after Descartes's death, his physics was outdated, his notion of extension replaced by another, and concepts like those of substance or form that he had deemed obsolete, found themselves restored by Leibniz in a new interpretation. When modern philosophy was Descartes's philosophy, it would have been necessary to construct a Cartesian theology even if it meant replacing it by a Leibnizian theology twenty years later. What other theology would have seemed legitimated by the philosophy of the day? I see one of them completely constructed, that of Nicholas Malebranche, a priest of the Oratory. Moreover, there have been innumerable Malebranchean theologians. In the eighteenth century, the Piedmontese theologian and philosopher

16

Segismond Gerdil still offered an admirable summary of Malebranche's doctrines, which is a model of its kind. But the basis of Malebranchism is that "God alone is cause." There are no second causes except occasional causes, because they are completely lacking in efficacy. Who would teach such a doctrine today? Nobody. Yet another theology would thus be needed to replace that one, but which theology? Excellent Christians, not just lay Catholics but priests, proposed Kant. Fr. Louis Bautain, theology professor at Strasbourg, especially recommended Kant, because according to this philosopher, *there are no possible demonstrations of the existence of God.* Moral conscience and faith alone remain. Let us suppose that this theology had triumphed. Where would we be today? I see no problem with anyone thinking this way for himself and in what concerns him, but I would see great problems in anyone wanting to impose this theology on that of the Church. Not only do I think that there are positive philosophical reasons to affirm God's existence, but I find it inconceivable that God should not exist. I know atheists exist or people who think they are atheists, but for my part, I have a very simple means of situating my reason in the presence of the philosophical problem of God: it is to ask myself how it happens that anything exists. I will be told that this is not a problem, and indeed it is not a scientific problem, because if nothing existed there would not be science or scientists, nothing to know, nor anyone to know it. But it is a metaphysical problem, the very one that Leibniz, one of the creators of modern mathematics, posed in unforgettable terms: "Why is there something rather than nothing?" Martin Heidegger, the most metaphysical mind of our time, has gone back over this expression several times and adds, always with Leibniz: "All the more because nothingness is easier."

I give you this last clause of the sentence to occupy yourself with in bed, before going to sleep. What I keep saying in this regard stays the same: who today would be content with Kantian theology? Nobody. After Kant we would have had a Hegelian theology, a Bergsonian theology, a Blondelian theology, as there has been in Italy a Giobertian theology, a more or less Gentilian theology, and so on indefinitely. Perhaps you ask me what is wrong with that. Simply this. Christian theology is an interpretation of Christian faith in the truth of God's word, which does not change. It is not necessary that this should be a scholarly interpretation. Our beloved father, Pope John XXIII, told me one day: "For me, you know, theology is 'Our

Father who art in heaven...'" So it is for all of us, but to say "Our Father" is to profess that we believe in one God, the all-powerful father and, whatever our theology may be, to be Christian it necessarily must line up with our belief in the God of the gospel. No theology that fails to profess this truth can call itself Christian. The one that best sheds light on this truth of faith and all those that the credo proclaims will obviously be the best, most perfect, and most completely true theology of the Church. The Church has simply proclaimed that the theology in which she recognizes the most faithful interpretation of the faith of which she has the deposit, the responsibility, and the custody, is St. Thomas Aquinas's.

I already know the objection: but then you want to lead us back to Aristotle's philosophy. As an eminent prelate recently said: "Dialogue with the Middle Ages is not dialogue with today's world." I come out in agreement with that, but I would like to make two remarks.

First, although the word *dialogue* is fashionable, I distrust it a little. Two are needed to dialogue. As far back as I go in my past, I see myself as enthusiastically open to my time as it was possible to be. I immediately thought that, having to do philosophy, it was first necessary to learn what already existed. So I devoted a large part of my life to study and teaching history of philosophy, and I do not regret it. I have read almost all the great works of ancient and modern western philosophy, published books on Descartes, written in part and directed a general history of philosophy. Excuse this catalogue, but what I want to say is that if I am ready to talk with others about their philosophies, it suffices that I wish to talk to them about Thomism for them to tell me with a pleasant smile: "Yes, yes, that is very interesting. You are very right to draw attention to him." But I would be curious to know in how many of my contemporaries I have inspired the curiosity of themselves reading any of the writings of Thomas Aquinas. I do not believe that my case is unique. It is their time that refuses to dialogue with Thomists. It is not Thomists who refuse to dialogue with their time.

My second comment is that nobody intends to lead our contemporaries back to the thirteenth century, neither to its science nor its philosophy. I understand that we are no longer in the epoch of Aristotle's qualitative physics or of Greek geocentric astronomy. But to what science shall we turn? Newton's is out-dated. Einstein's is now included in a more general vision of nature, and as for cosmography, with quasars we are at the edge of a breathtaking revolution in our conception of the universe. But what relation is there between the Thomism that the Church tells us to follow and any sort of science? All the Church wants us to accept in this matter is that God created the world from nothing. This is not a scientific proposition. Science has no way of knowing whether it is true or it is not. If it is true, the universe created by God is the one science knows in the measure in which it knows it. In relation to the theological notion of creation, all of science's successive universes are equivalent. In other words, the universe that God created is the one science has described, whatever he is and it is.

What is true about science is true about philosophy. Doctrines succeed each other so rapidly that when we accept one as true, we can be sure it will cease to be true before long. When I was twenty

Credette Bergson nella filosofia
tener lo campo, ed ora ha Heidegger il grido
sí che la fama di colui è oscura.

[Bergson thought to hold the field in philosophy,
and now Heidegger has the cry,
so that the fame of the other is obscured.][1]

This movement of philosophy corresponds to a need as real as that of science, but the Church wanted to establish a testimonial theology, an immutable center of reference, because, while all the rest changes, the truth she guards does not change.

This truth is that of the word of God, of which Scripture said, heaven and earth will pass away, but the word of God will not pass away. Here I

---

1 [Translator: My Fitchburg State University colleague Rala Diakité points out that this is a play on Dante, *Purgatorio* Canto XI, vv. 94–96. I have adapted the English of those lines from the bilingual edition of the *Purgatorio*, p. 133, London: Dent and New York: Dutton, 1901, thirteenth edition, 1933, reprinted 1952: The original is:

Cimabue thought to hold the field in painting,
and now Giotto hath the cry, so that the fame
of the other is obscured.]

think that we Christians, philosophers, or theologians, or both, have to look at ourselves, because I greatly fear that we are guilty of having piled up illusions and multiplied useless difficulties for ourselves and others.

We have said and repeated in every key during centuries that St. Thomas's philosophy was Aristotle's. Those who said it, came to make it be believed and worst of all believed it themselves. Many still believe it today, to such a degree that they hold almost heretical the proposition, nonetheless evident, that the philosophy of St. Thomas Aquinas *is not* that of Aristotle. The language is the same, the technique in demonstration is similar, but the doctrine's content is different. Leaving aside every properly theological consideration, Aristotle does teach that there is only one God, that God is pure act of being, that he created the world from nothing, that he conserves it in its actual existence itself, that God is thereby intimately present in everything that is, that he created man in his image and likeness, that God's image in man is the intellect, that the end of the intellect is to see God, that the human soul is immortal and consequently capable of eternal beatitude. About all that, which St. Thomas teaches, Aristotle knew nothing, and if Aristotle equals philosophy, philosophy knows nothing about it.

So what did St. Thomas Aquinas do? He said it and said it again, but it is still a point about which Domingo Báñez's phrase can be repeated: *et hoc est quod saepissime clamat divus Thomas, et Thomistae nolunt audire*. He particularly said it at the start of that *Summa Contra Gentiles*, which, nevertheless, is so often labeled *philosophical*. "We first strive to make evident the truth that faith professes, and that reasons submits to scrutiny. We will propose some demonstrations and some probable reasons for it, certain of which we will gather in the writings of philosophers and Christians in order to confirm truth and convince the adversary" (*Summa Contra Gentiles*, I, 9).[2] Thomas did not construct his doctrine by meditating on Aristotle but by meditating on Holy Scripture, doubtless with the help of Aristotle's philosophy but also of all the philosophical truth at his disposal, and, above all, of all his own reason could discover.

---

2   [Tr. *Summa Contra Gentiles* I, 9, "Modo ergo proposito procedere intendentes, primum nitemur ad manifestationem illius veritatis quam fides profitetur et ratio investigat, inducentes rationes demonstrativas et probabiles, quarum quasdam ex libris philosophorum et Sanctorum collegimus, per quas veritas confirmetur et adversarius convincatur."]

But, it will be said, this is theology. Assuredly, and St. Thomas never pretended it was anything else. Then, it will be objected, it is not philosophy. Why would it not be? Why would a theologian be incapable of using his reason as well as a philosopher? Why would he cease to use it correctly and legitimately from the moment at which, believing something on God's word, he wonders in all tranquility and freedom: what do I know about this thing we believe? If he knows nothing about it, he will say, "I know nothing about it," and will continue to believe it. If he believes he knows something, he will say, "That is what I know about it," and will continue to believe the rest. It was by asking himself what he knew about what he believed that St. Thomas constituted this body of rational demonstrated truths that today we call St. Thomas Aquinas's philosophy.

It is understandable from this that the Church should recognize a privileged authority for this philosophy and for the theology of which it is part, and a permanent value that it does not acknowledge for any other.

The Church does not dispute anyone's right to philosophize in his manner. She has no opinion about symbolic or other logic, about philosophy of science, or about any philosophical doctrine in general. At least she does not as long as these doctrines do not present themselves, or are not presented by overzealous admirers, as expressing the truths that the Church herself acknowledges as her own or that she can take under her own responsibility. Those responsible for the majority of doctrinal condemnations are not the authors of the doctrines in dispute, but those who obstinately maintain that they represent the truth of faith or are a legitimate interpretation of it. By dint of maintaining that a doctrine is orthodox, they inevitably succeed in getting it censured.

What can we do then? I would simply ask those who deny Thomas any present philosophical value, how much time they have devoted to studying him. If they have made the necessary effort, if they are certain of having understood the doctrine well and not of having unconsciously substituted for it one of the numerous versions revised and corrected by his interpreters, then the case has been heard, Thomism is not made for them. There are other philosophies better suited to their needs.

To others, among whom am I, for whom Thomism constitutes their preferred and familiar intellectual nourishment, I would permit myself to give just one piece of advice: take it as it is and present it as it is, without trying to make it pass for something else. The worse thing we could do is to disguise it as a philosophy of nature without any link to the religious faith that St. Thomas, a preaching friar, made his study every day and almost every hour. Those who change features of St. Thomas in the hope of winning adepts for Christianity through the paths of philosophy, whatever my sympathy might be for the goal that they set, seem to me to take a bad path to attain it. God does not propose to save men by Aristotle's doctrine but by his own word. It is by meditation upon that word as a philosopher that Thomas Aquinas has led metaphysics much further than Aristotle. So much further, that the best of our own contemporaries no longer even meet him there. For me, I find him very much ahead of the boldest of those in whose company I have been invited to leave him behind. I cannot conceive that one could follow him to the completion of his luminous metaphysics of the act of being without feeling the desire to remain there with him always.

II

St. Thomas Now

We cannot discuss St. Thomas without noticing that no consensus prevails about the man and the body of work that bears his name. Naturally, the same holds for the terms "Thomism" and finally for the label "Thomist." To review the ways of understanding these words, very widely used today, would be a vast labor of little profit, all the more because each different acceptation of these terms rests on a different way of understanding the doctrine of the Church's Common Doctor. It seems more useful to me to limit my effort to clarifying what Thomist doctrine means for me and thereby to give some idea of the reasons that a twentieth-century person might still have to make the perusal of a thirteenth century thinker's writings not only his work but his pleasure. For those who identify with St. Thomas's teaching, it is a duty of intellectual honesty to explain themselves on this point. The multitude of philosophers who oppose Thomistic philosophy, and even any Scholastic philosophy in general, in the event that they care, have the right to know what the doctrine is they reject without having studied it personally. As for those who identify with the tradition of the School, and even with that of St. Thomas, they understand each other about Thomism with all the more difficulty because, holding it *grosso modo* as what in their eyes is the expression of the truth of Catholicism itself, the slightest differences of interpretation assume importance disproportionate to their real scope. In the end, we all have the duty to fly our colors, as sailors say, not without expecting to receive the first cannon balls when our adversaries recognize them.

I start with a proposition that appears inoffensive but is effectively revolutionary: St. Thomas is in fact and above all a theologian. His masterpiece, the *Summa Theologiae,* bears a title, which is fairly self-explanatory. A second exposition of his overall doctrine bears the no less clear title of *Compendium Theologiae.* Both of these works are unfinished, but there is a

23

summa that its author did finish, known by the title *Summa Contra Gentiles*, which some distinguish from the summa called theological by naming it the "philosophical summa." St. Thomas never used that title. The title given by several old manuscripts, *De Veritate Fidei Contra Errores Infidelium*, insists a little too much on the work's polemical side but expresses its content fairly well. The still simpler title Bernardus Maria de Rubeis gave it, *De Veritate Fidei Catholicae*, seems quite accurate. What could be clearer? A summa of Catholic truth is theological by definition. An author whose doctrine is expressed in three works of theology is essentially a theologian. But, I will be asked, what about the rest? Everything else, disputed questions, opuscula, commentaries on Dionysius, Boethius, Proclus, and even Aristotle, represent an effort that Thomas had to take on in order to be able to construct his great doctrinal synthesis. His entire activity as a philosopher was undertaken, pursued, and carried to fruition in view of his work as a theologian. Therefore, if I am asked what I call *Thomism*, I will answer, it is a theology, because the author's whole activity was either theological or ordered toward the goals of theology. And if someone persists in asking me how I know that, my answer will be that St. Thomas himself said so. Appropriating an expression of St. Hilary of Poitiers, the author of our alleged philosophical summa declares in chapter two, "I am aware that my chief duty to God in this life is that all my words and all my thoughts should be about him." I do not think I exaggerate at all in saying that when all of a person's words and thoughts deal with God and when this person wanted to do that for his whole life, he is essentially a theologian.

But what did Thomas understand by the term theology? In his eyes, it was a sacred science resting above all on God's word. He defined this knowledge at the beginning of the *Summa Theologiae*, or rather — I cannot overemphasize the point —he took a description from St. Augustine: a science entirely devoted to study, clarify, and confirm God's word, not of course in itself, for it suffices unto itself, but according to the needs of humans, to dispose them to accept the faith. Thomistic theology simply desires to start anew the labor already carried out by St. Augustine, and there was much to do. We are not as distant in time from St. Thomas as he was from St. Augustine, but an *aggiornamento* of theology was necessary to take into account the considerable theological activity carried on during nine centuries: Gregory the Great, Hilary of Poitiers, Boethius, Anselm of Canterbury, and others. Philosophical activity had especially intensified. Aristotle's doctrine had taken hold of the schools and minds to such a degree that many considered it identical to philosophy itself. For theology to be taught in the thirteenth century it was necessary to shape it as a science in the Aristotelian mode, utilizing Aristotelian demonstrative techniques as much as possible. The issue was a new presentation of traditional theology, rather than a theology whose content would be new.

Accordingly, Thomistic theology wanted to be the heir of perennial theology. At bottom, it could not be otherwise. The substance of theological truth can only be the truths of Scripture and of dogma defined by the Councils. Elaborated by the Church Fathers of whom Augustine was the greatest but not the only one, this same truth is re-encountered in almost all theologies, although sometimes in slightly different terms. So St. Thomas simply wanted to put this doctrinal body in order but not change it. Everyone knows what difference there is between looking for what St. Augustine says about the existence of God and what St. Thomas Aquinas says about it. Whereas what St. Augustine says is scattered across several works bearing on different topics, it is enough to go to *Summa Contra Gentiles*, I, 13, or to the *Summa Theologiae*. I, 2, 3, to find the essence of what St. Thomas said on the question.

In a certain sense, it follows that there is no theology peculiar to St. Thomas Aquinas. He did not write a summa of *his* theology but a summa of *theology*, where what is essential in the sacred science would be gathered, set in order, and explained as simply as possible for use by beginners. Certainly, his own contribution is essential: plan, order of subjects, demonstrative method, and above all the articulation of certain key, very personal concepts, to which we see clearly that he attached great importance; for example, his concept of the act of being or *esse*. But he did not organize theology around these notions to the point of rendering it inseparable from them. The proof is that certain Thomisms, like that of Cajetan, easily dispenses with those concepts. They have even made very ingenious efforts to conserve St. Thomas's whole theology except his principles. Many Suarezians consider themselves Thomists, although their peculiar doctrine in regard to method and certain principles differs perceptibly from St. Thomas Aquinas's. To state as briefly as possible something whose clarification would require a great deal of time and which perhaps only long acquaintance with the doctrine allows one to comprehend, St. Thomas

Aquinas's theology is of such a nature and animated with such a spirit that it accommodates several other theologies, sometimes as they stand, other times at the cost of a little touching up, but doing complete justice to what truth they contain.

This is particularly true in what concerns St. Augustine's doctrine. Of Augustinianism it can be said that its entire substance has been passed into the *Summa Theologiae*. When St. Thomas cannot accept Augustine's literal statement, he takes care to make us see how the same idea can be formulated differently. For example, let us take the philosophically crucial problem of the mode of human knowledge. Do we know the truth in the light of our intellect or do we know it in a divine light added to that of the intellect? The Middle Ages saw interminable controversies on this point, and of course Thomas Aquinas took a position on the question. He judged that humans know truth, even eternal truths, in the light of their own agent intellects. But when it is objected to him that St. Augustine requires an intervention of the divine light, Thomas responds that there is no great difference between saying that we know the truth in the divine light, or saying that we know it in the light of our intellect, which in us is the mark left by God upon his creature. In the last analysis, humans always know truth in the divine light. The philosophical difference that separates the two theses loses much of its importance when it is seen from the height of theological wisdom. In both cases it is humans who know, and they only know thanks to the divine light. The doctrine's philosophical adjustment has its importance for the theologian who philosophizes, but he has no reason to exclude one of them precisely insofar as what interests him is the truth of faith.

Here I arrive at what seems to me to be the central point of the debate. What strikes me most forcefully in my contacts with theologies other than Thomism, but whose orthodoxy is not doubtful, is that each of them seems to me to be called to make evident an important, even necessary, moment of the whole truth: St. Augustine and his dialectic of time and of truth, St. Gregory of Nyssa and Dionysius and their negative theology, St. Anselm and his unshakable confidence in the necessity of reason reasoning [*ratio ratiocinans*], St. Bonaventure whose metaphysical meditation attains the level of mystical contemplation with unique ease, Blessed John Duns Scotus and his metaphysics of essences that so felicitously opens onto a theology of infinite being. I set them aside without forgetting them, and the better

I know them, the more I am convinced of the necessity of some and the usefulness of all. When I am told that no single theology is adequate to the total truth of the divine word, I am already deeply convinced of that and I believe I can say that I grasp the reasons for it. I would go further: the total truth of all patristic, medieval or modern, Latin or Greek theologies is not adequate to the word of God to which theology aspires to be mere commentary, clarification, and the doorway. The observation holds for Thomas Aquinas as for other theologians. The immense difference I find between him and others is that he always lets me comprehend the truth of their particular theologies and consequently gives access to it, whereas none of these theologies let me comprehend Thomas's. I have never written a single page against the theology of St. Augustine, St. Anselm, St. Bonaventure, or Blessed John Duns Scotus. They are too well-know to me to feel the slightest desire to do so. What astounds me is firstly to see these great theologies criticized, condemned and, as is the case of John Duns Scotus, sometimes literally slandered by adversaries who claim the authority of St. Thomas Aquinas. What astonishes me at least as much is to see St. Thomas's theology judged and condemned in its turn by certain partisans — in the worst sense of the term — of these other theologies, who think they can only subsist on condition of suppressing Thomas's theology first. I will permit myself to not cite examples of these painful controversies whose adversaries exchange accusations that shine neither in charity nor intelligence. Finally, if someone preaches harmony, he is naturally accused of doctrinal indifference and skepticism. All adversaries pile upon him.

The only interesting thing about these disputes is to understand why they are possible. They are possible because, when St. Thomas set out to achieve a synthesis of all human wisdom, philosophical and theological, whether by good fortune, by the vision of genius, or by personal favor of heaven, he almost immediately put his finger upon a first principle. This first principle was such that it could not be included in any other and that all conceivable principles should necessarily be included in it. Let us add that this principle can include others without making them lose anything of their specificity. I am aware of being too abstract at this instant, but we are at the peak of metaphysical abstraction. I can really only excuse myself and try to remedy the difficulty at the risk of making it worse.

The first principle of Thomas is the concept of being, understood in its properly Thomistic sense of "that which has the act of existing." This point dominates all others, because, whatever the other of which you speak may be, if it does not exist, it is not a being, it is nothing. Some prefer a philosophy of the one or the good or the true or essence or relation or everything else of this kind, but unless they exist, the one, the good, the true, or the essence is nothing. Unless a relation is established between actual beings, it is only a relation between two nothings. Lastly, if the famous composition of act and potency is not the composition of a being in act and a being in potency, it only composes as between two nothings. So it is not surprising that St. Thomas should successively appeal to these different principles of intelligibility to explain the real under the different aspects it presents, because all are legitimate as founded upon the transcendental unity of the act of being. It is similarly understandable that Thomism does not feel disoriented in other doctrines that invoke one or another of the transcendentals, of the fundamental properties of being. What they say is true, even if they do not tell the whole truth, and, since some minds are particularly sensitive to one or another of its particular moments, it is good that certain doctrines put these moments in evidence. Only, those who see all these moments in the unity of the same principle experience no difficulty in doing them justice, while those who see the world from the point of view of a particular principle, or one less general than the only properly universal one, will naturally be tempted to deny or ignore the others, as if the only valid point of view were theirs.

The first principle, which is called *being* in philosophy, is called *God* in theology. To conceive God as the act of pure being and first cause and goal of all other being is also to give oneself a theory capable of doing justice to what all the other theologies can possess of truth, just as the metaphysics of *esse* has the way of doing justice to what other philosophies can possess of truth. Because it includes them all, this theology of the act of being, or of the God whose proper name is *I Am*, is as true as all together can be and more true than any one of them separately. If I am not mistaken, this is the secret reason of the choice the Church has made of Thomas Aquinas as its Common Doctor and the patron of all schools where the doctrine of salvation is taught. I cannot pretend that this rule does not contradict some preferences, but it does not threaten any freedom. If what a master teaches, in whatever way he justifies it, can be validated by the authentic principles of Thomistic theology, what he teaches is true. We can only request him to be prepared to tolerate that others, who think they can justify that truth better than he does himself, do so. To one who hesitates to follow him, St. Thomas's disciple will gladly repeat Beatrice's words to Dante (*Paradiso*, canto V, lines 10–12):

> *E s'altra cosa vostro amore seduce,*
> > *non è se non di quella alcun vestigio,*
> > *mal conosciuto, che quivi traluce.*
> [And if aught else seduce your love, naught is it
> > save some vestige of this light, ill understood,
> > that shineth through therein.][1]

There are many mansions in the Father's house. The important thing is that everyone be sheltered under the same roof.

The impatience many people show when someone speaks to them about following St. Thomas Aquinas stems first of all from a misunderstanding for which the Thomists are often as responsible as their adversaries. It is natural and normal that many friends of philosophy only wish to get what it can in fact give: knowledge of the world in the light of first principles of natural reason. As long as they do not claim to speak in the name of the Church and of Christian truth, which would be to present their personal doctrine as a legitimate interpretation of the word of God as the Church believes and teaches it, I think that the Church will not care much about what they please to say. The Church is only interested in philosophy evidently in the measure in which it combats the Church's teaching or, on the contrary, offers itself as being itself either the Church's teaching or its legitimate interpretation. Christians in search of a rational interpretation of their faith cannot therefore avoid posing the question: is this new view of the world that has been proposed to me more satisfying for my reason and faith than Thomism is? If it is, no hesitation is possible, but if it is not, what reason could I have to accept it?

To understand the exceptional, unique status the Church gives St. Thomas, it is therefore always necessary to remember the exceptional,

---

1   Dante, *Paradiso*, Dent: London, 1899, 14th edition, 1931, reprinted 1954, p. 49.

unique nature of the work he achieved, not a task carried out with personal goals in mind, but an effort to give an overview, valid for all Christians, *de veritate fidei catholicae*. To understand the sense of this work, we must know it, and when we see what objections are directed against it, we are obliged to ask ourselves whether their authors have ever pursued their studies beyond some so-called Thomistic school textbooks to the writings of St. Thomas himself.

At the level of theology properly speaking, an odd objection, whose origin I do not know, has recently begun to gather impetus and spread in high places. I take its formulation from a release by the press office of the Second Vatican Council (or Vatican II, because there seems to be a habit of numbering Councils like the artificial satellites with which communists and capitalists strive to populate the heavens). *Le Devoir* of Montreal gave it to the public on November 16, 1964: "Furthermore, it would be an error to impose the Scholastic philosophical system on non-western minds. The Council's task is not to furnish a philosophical system but only to offer general directives. St. Thomas might well be an example and model without thereby imposing his system. Our seminarians ought to imitate his mentality that impelled him to use science to help the spread of the Gospel."

Once more I allow myself to protest the basic confusion between philosophy and theology for which Thomists themselves are largely responsible. We see it at work here with pernicious consequences. Certainly, there is philosophy in Thomism. I have said, written, and repeated many times that in my eyes Thomism sets the mark for the summit of metaphysical speculation and that, in this regard, it is ahead of the existentialism that is regarded nowadays as the cutting edge of philosophical reflection. If I had time, I would even say or try to say why its primacy will never be wrested from Thomism. However, if as they say, the Church imposes a system, it cannot be any philosophical system as such. Augustine, Gregory the Great, Hilary of Poitiers, Bonaventure, Duns Scotus, and Ockham have all been either Fathers of the Church, or ecclesiastical writers, or masters in theology. Since the Scholastic method in theology consists of proposing an understanding of faith, philosophy nourishes all these theologies though they remain no less theologies. Thomas Aquinas's case is exactly the same. Supposing, as they say, that the Church wants to impose him, this could only be under the heading of theology. Whatever philosophy is included is there insofar as employed by theology at its service and as an instrument of intellection of the faith. Thus, if we wanted to replace Thomism, it would not be enough to substitute another philosophy for it—that would be easy, because philosophy never stops changing. It would be necessary to find another philosophy as capable as Thomism of expressing the truth of the word of God in intelligible terms. That is certainly what St. Thomas, following and accompanying St. Augustine, proposed to do. In a time when Scholastic theology is regarded with suspicion by the partisans of what they call "biblical" or even "evangelical" theology, it is strange to have to recall that all of St. Thomas's theology is a commentary on the Bible. He puts no conclusion forward without justifying it by some word of scripture, which is the word of God. If we really want to admit that the Church is qualified to say in what theology she recognizes the most faithful expression of its own teaching, she certainly does not exceed her powers, she does not go beyond her proper function by recommending Thomism as a doctrinal norm that even those who do not follow it are invited to at least respect.

The idea that such a norm ought not be applied to those who are termed "non-western" only worsens the predicament of those who pass for Thomists or consider themselves such. More than forty years ago the editor of a Paris weekly invited me as a Thomist to enroll in a new crusade for the *Defense of the West*. Between us, I am quite sure that some of my friends still break lances today for this noble cause. I regretted having to excuse myself. "How so," I was told, "you are a Thomist!" To which I responded, "Yes, exactly because I am a Thomist!" Let us reason a little. St. Thomas Aquinas was a Christian, a disciple of Jesus Christ born at Bethlehem, a town situated on the wrong side of the Mediterranean for the Occidentalists. For us other westerners, salvation comes from the East. Auguste Comte said that Christianity's true founder was not Jesus Christ but St. Paul. Let us grant that to the first and last Positivist pope without believing it. St. Paul was born at Tarsus and his preaching brought him to Antioch before taking him to Rome, the site of his martyrdom. Here again, to want to protect Christianity from the Orient is to defend Christianity against itself. What about Thomas himself? It is impossible to conceive his theology, just as it is, without taking into account the speculation of the Greek Fathers, Dionysius, Origen, Clement of Alexandria, Basil, Gregory of Nyssa, Gregory Nazianzen, in short all who are called the great Cappadocians.

Cappadocia was a province of Asia Minor. St. John Damascene was St. John of Damascus. None of these places is in the West, and yet none of these theologies failed to leave their mark on the teaching of the *Summa Theologiae*. Since dialogue is the fashion, I see no Western theology better qualified to dialogue with the Greek rite Churches than Thomas Aquinas's theology.

Yes, it will be objected, but it is this theology's philosophy that concerns us. I agree, but then I find myself in the obligation to recall that the Aristotle Thomas puts at the service of his theology is the Aristotle of the Oriental philosopher Avicenna, born in Iran, near Bukhara, a city in Asia, and that the only interpreter of Aristotle who challenged Avicenna in his thought was another Muslim, Averroes, a Spanish Arab, whom it will be difficult to view as a witness for the West. In reality, it is because, thanks to Albert the Great and Thomas Aquinas, to name only the two greatest, that the medieval West amply opened itself to the East, and that we have a Western tradition to defend today. Why would Thomism separate today what Thomas Aquinas joined? Those who express such fears construct a strange idea of the history of Western civilization. Those acquainted with it know too well what it owes to the East to ever be tempted to separate them.

Still, a question haunts the thought of lay philosophers who are reproached, often bitterly, for wanting to perpetuate the teaching of Thomism in an epoch when that doctrine is manifestly outdated: where, then, is Thomism taught? If by Thomism we understand the doctrine of St. Thomas, I would say: in Christian schools very seldom, outside Christian schools, the only ones to which Pope Leo XIII directed the encyclical *Aeterni Patris*, absolutely nowhere. In Christian schools they teach manuals of philosophy and theology conceived *ad mentem divi Thomae Aquinatis*. These are often very well done, but so different among themselves that an overall judgment cannot be formulated, and even if his doctrine is still more or less present in them, St. Thomas himself is absent. There is no shadow of blame in what I say, because I gladly recognize that it is practically impossible in the twentieth century to initiate students into philosophy and even into Christian theology by plunging them into the works of St. Thomas Aquinas from the outset. We are no longer in Aristotle's world. Nor are we in the world of St. Thomas. Seven centuries of science, philosophy, and art, of which he knew nothing and could foresee nothing, separate us from him today. Literature, press, and radio teach our students a different philosophical language from that of the school, without even try-ing to. I happily grant all that and even many other things, but they have no bearing on the question. Again, we have lost sight of the issue; it is nat-ural that there should be many philosophies and that they change contin-ually. St. Thomas often repeated it: philosophy has as its object nature seen in the light of reason. We will add that the nature upon which philosophy reflects changes in the measure in which the science we possess about nature changes. The theologian, by contrast, directs his reflections toward the word of God, which does not change. Therefore, to substitute a new theology for that of St. Thomas, it would be necessary to discover a deeper, more solid, more faithful interpretation of the word of God. The Church does not say that it is impossible. She only says that, until now, she does not know one, and, as she is responsible for the word of God, she invites us all not to discard the surest interpreter of it that she knows. The Church re-mains faithful to her role. She cannot be blamed for it.

Here perhaps we come to touch upon the confusion that vitiates the whole controversy. Because St. Thomas appealed to the philosophy of his time to obtain a certain understanding of the word of God, we are invited to do the same thing by appealing to the philosophy of our time. That is something easier said than done. To use science "to promote the spread of the Gospel" is not a project of work that corresponds to seminarians. It cor-responds rather to the greatest of their masters, and the project could really only be carried out by new Thomas Aquinases. We can even ask whether the task is still possible in our days. In their time, Albert the Great and Thomas Aquinas were the best philosophers: *praecipui in philosophia, Albertus et Thomas.* So spoke their adversary Siger of Brabant, and indeed they could outdo the most famous Aristotelians of their time on Aristotle. But it is not conceivable today that a theologian, even a genius, should also be one of the greatest mathematicians, astronomers, physicists, biologists, or sociologists of his time. Today, to be a scientist no longer consists in knowing what there is in Aristotle, but what there is in the world. No single human suffices. All we can say is that the more the world of science is revealed to be great and wondrous, the more the admiration for its Author should increase in us. Whatever image of the world science offers us, that should always be true. If that is what we want to do, we can, because it will always be something to do over again, with or without St. Thomas Aquinas's help.

In any case, the important thing is to understand that it is not what Thomas himself did. If that is what we want to do, we will not redo what he did. We will do something else, because Thomas did not interpret the word of God in the light of the science of his time. It is true that descending from the word of God toward God's works at each step, so to speak, the theologian encounters the scientist and the philosopher, who are elevating themselves from their knowledge of nature toward that of its causes. But like those who go up and down the same stairway, even when they meet, their movements are not in the same direction. At all times, whatever the state of human knowledge may be, the theologian's approach remains the same: it does not consist in discovering God starting from science, but starting from the word of God to know God. On this subject, the admirable first chapter of *Summa Contra Gentiles* book IV can never be read too often. To redo today what Thomas Aquinas did is not to hurl ourselves with bowed head among the philosophies of our time in the hope of rediscovering the truth we are seeking at the end. It is to descend again from revealed truth toward the philosophies of our time to clarify them, purify them, and finally restore them to themselves in the fullness of their truth. The task is immense, but Thomas Aquinas preceded us in it and can still lead us. While we are not indebted to him for a science better than Aristotle's, we have inherited from him a metaphysics by whose light we can always proceed to that transcendental critique of the scientific views of the world which succeed each other in the course of the centuries. This metaphysics, a philosophy germinated in a Christian climate in the soil of the divine word, is what the Church asks us to maintain. Why should we be surprised at this? Whether Christians believe to know or know to believe, the intelligences of Christians who philosophize will always philosophize in faith.

This is what St. Thomas Aquinas did, and it is what gives his doctrine its perennial relevance. There are all kinds of current events. In newspapers, we call current events what is happening or has just happened but has only momentary interest. What is current today will not be so tomorrow. By contrast, Thomism is perennially current. Popes have recommended it to the faithful as current for more than six centuries. Those who are surprised that such a phenomenon is possible only show that they do not understand what is unique in the execution and conception of St. Thomas's undertaking.

As *intellectus fidei*, Scholastic theology concerns the deposit of faith just as we receive it from revelation and tradition. This deposit is exactly the object of Thomistic reflection. It must remain the object of our tradition today, and that is why our theology and St. Thomas's have exactly the same object. Every new theology where we do not immediately acknowledge the God of the Old Testament and the Christ of the Gospels as its principal object, ought to be suspect for us from the outset. Since St. Thomas's whole theology concerns first and always the articles of faith or their preambles, it must always be contemporary in the Church. In a way, by definition it is always contemporary, since its task is to define what cannot change in the Church's teaching.

Thomas's theology is still contemporary, because of the perennial character of the principles to which it appeals to achieve a satisfactory understanding of that faith. These are not those of physics, biology, experimental psychology, nor any of the positive sciences, which never stop changing. The parts of Thomism linked to a scientific picture of the universe that is now outdated cannot be maintained in an era where they have obviously ceased to be true. The same does not hold for Thomistic metaphysics, which consists of an interpretation of the first principles and particularly of the first principle. Those who desire another theology implicitly admit that the notion of being is not the first principle of the human mind, or that a metaphysician of genius who came after St. Thomas has pushed the interpretation of *ens* conceived as what has *esse* further than Thomas did. I do not see this metaphysician. I see many philosophers who have turned their back on metaphysics or who have more or less voluntarily ignored St. Thomas's metaphysics or who having followed it just so far cannot stand its light. For those who live by it, the Common Doctor's metaphysics accepted in its fullness is a *nec plus ultra* of the understanding. At the same time, unsurpassable in itself and inexhaustible in its consequences, it is the human understanding itself in its permanent tasks of rational interpretation of man and the world. The more the spirit faithfully adheres to its principles, the more it is free in its interpretation of consequences; because its rule of understanding is as immutable as its object, this theology's contemporary character is perennial and permanent, only manifesting once more *sacra doctrina* in its very essence: *velut quaedam impressio divinae scientiae, quae est una et simplex omnium.*

35

III

In the Land of Shadows

Old age offers fewer benefits than the author of the treatises *De Senectute* claimed, but it banishes the frequent illusion of youth that we are witnessing events such as have never been seen. When an itinerant Thomist presents himself to an audience new to him, he knows well that his presence is received in different ways. Those who invited him desire a lecture or two on St. Thomas, whether in deference toward the Church's Common Doctor or out of curiosity about a doctrine little or not at all known that hopefully a good lecturer will help them polish off in an hour. But in the audience there are also young people with the insatiable curiosity that is the very spark of life and a burning desire to let nothing be lost of the good things that their own time offers in profusion, one might almost say, on their behalf. I think I am not mistaken in feeling that behind courtesy tinged with indulgence for someone visibly belonging to a different epoch, there is regret. Such a person seems to linger over the past instead of speaking to people, who do belong to the present, about philosophers or doctrines that also belong to the present.

They are right. One can only enter philosophy by the philosophy of one's own time. That philosophy precedes us and comes to us from all directions, be it only in the daily paper and books. When we become aware of its presence, it is already in place, and even if education undertakes to chase it away, that struggle confirms the philosophy's existence. How many doctrines have been propagated by refuting them! The confusion between the concepts of novelty and progress, often justified in the natural sciences but so deceptive in philosophy, greatly adds to the attraction the latest philosophies exercise upon our minds. When a young audience is faced with a spokesman for a thirteenth-century theologian who still believed that the earth is immobile and situated at the center of the physical universe and that the number of living species is the same today as on the day of creation, that audience thinks they are being made fun of and is tempted to make fun of the bearer of an outdated message.

Later on, when we see the trajectory of those formerly bright stars, now burned out or in the process of burning out, we wonder whether a sort of law does not condemn everything to the same fate. It is not without interest to ponder the reasons for this fact.

When I was studying philosophy at the Sorbonne, no opposition set religion and metaphysics in conflict. Had the question been posed, the only point upon which our professors would have insisted was that the two orders ought to be kept separate. That was completely reasonable in a public university where one could only keep all religions away or accept them all. How might they all be accepted without setting the different truths of faith at odds, irreconcilable by ordinary philosophical methods? Insofar as religion invokes something beyond rational knowledge, it goes out of the philosophical domain, even if the latter is in the transcendent.

So we lived under a regime of separation of philosophy and religion, as France lived under that of separation of Church and State. We did not have to suffer from that. Students have all philosophy to study, philosophy of science, of nature, and of human nature before committing themselves to the badly defined terrain of philosophy of religion. This regime did not even include natural theology, held by Aristotle to be the culmination of philosophy, and which still opens unlimited perspectives today for philosophical reflection. Thus, the situation was rational and respectful for all sorts of freedoms.

A difficulty still remains, which stemmed from the very natural desire felt by Christian philosophers to harmonize the absolutely philosophical natural theology with their supernatural theology, revealed and absolutely religious. Each of us was free to devote himself to this reconciliation, but we strongly felt that the term reconciliation would not suffice in the event. Dealing with God, who is everything for humans, simple arbitration between two ways of knowing and speaking of him could satisfy neither religious consciousness nor the need for unity that characterizes reason. The philosophers for whom religion was a living thing could not make do either with a religion "within the limits of reason" or with a religion extending metaphysics as hypotheses added on to science, where everyone more or less confusedly aspires to a sort of symbiosis of the two modes of knowledge. They desired that the term *god* should have the same meaning and designate the same object in the mind of the philosopher and of the believer.

The ambition is not only legitimate but also inevitable, and it still seeks satisfaction today. In France between 1905 and 1910, two philosophies appeared to offer satisfactory answers to this question. Unfortunately, they did not agree. They agreed so little that the second found its main justification in the insufficiency of the first.

Neo-Scholastic philosophy was the first possible solution. This philosophy had the great merit of existing and even of having a basic impact through teaching institutions that assured it and still assures it a kind of perpetuity. It had several labels: Scholastic or neo-Scholastic or again philosophy according to the mind of Thomas Aquinas or of Thomas and Aristotle. Many textbooks have presented it. Some had a dazzling success in Christian schools and major seminaries. Insofar as this philosophy presents itself as Thomist, it constitutes in some measure the Catholic Church's "offical" philosophy. So why would not Catholics in search of a philosophy be happy to accept it?

There is the fact that, if they accept it, they depart from the main current of philosophy of their time. Starting with Descartes, living philosophical speculation turned away from Scholasticism. After having been the main current for four centuries, Scholasticism suddenly found itself discredited, entangled in the insolvency of Greek science, especially in the Aristotelian form to which it had been tied since the thirteenth century. Modern astronomy displaced the center of the physical universe. The closed universe of celestial spheres burst and was extended indefinitely not to say infinitely. Nature defined by its forms was now controlled by number; quality yielded to quantity; everything was thereby submitted to computation. What was totally decisive, moreover, was the practical success of the new science following Aristotelianism's centuries old sterility. From the sixteenth century on, major scientific discoveries succeeded each other at an increasing rhythm until the explosion of Newtonian astronomy and its continuations. Now this prodigious movement of ideas, this almost unbelievable conquest of nature by humans, was not only produced outside Aristotle's doctrine but against it. Scholasticism was thus discredited simultaneously as philosophy and as science. It is still discredited today, and if it is not held up to ridicule today as Molière and Boileau did, it is because it has long ceased to be discussed. The idea that it would be necessary to profess Scholastic philosophy to have natural theology suiting the theology of Christian faith would hardly be popular today. Around 1905 nobody dreamed of it. Insofar as it included a philosophical crisis, modernism was there to bear witness to that.

Outside of Scholasticism, regarded as obsolete, the only doctrine in France offering a solution to the problem was Maurice Blondel's. The first published version of *L'Action* dates from 1893. A history of this thesis, first in its author's mind, then before the Sorbonne tribunal that had to judge it, would let us verify experimentally what the problem's data are. Lacking the time to involve myself in the detail of a complicated story that requires nuanced interpretation, I will attempt to say what this data seems to have been in the mind of Maurice Blondel.

Firstly, we are dealing with a thesis in philosophy, not at all in theology or apologetics. We will never know in what measure this corresponded to Blondel's own personal desire or represented a practical necessity imposed by the Sorbonne's secularism. The obstacle was real to such a degree that, presented in this way, the thesis had some difficulty in getting accepted. That is what Blondel meant to satisfy in his October 20, 1893 letter to Georges Perrot, Director of the École Normale Supérieur, in which he emphatically declared: "In intention and method my work is exclusively philosophical. It seems to me that it is so in the nature of the doctrine as in my conclusions."

Since intention, method, doctrine, and conclusions were philosophical, the work could rightly boast of being *exclusively* philosophical. Besides, Blondel is known to have wanted from the start to establish a Christian philosophy in the clearly religious sense of the expression. He extensively revamped his first project, but despite appearance to the contrary, he did not do so opportunistically. Early on, Blondel understood that the only possible way of serving religion through philosophy was to a establish a philosophy, strictly philosophical in method, nature, doctrine, and even in proximate intention, but whose conclusions would be of a nature such as to prepare access of minds to religion. When his conclusion formed in his own mind, the coincidence of practical possibilities and of rational philosophical necessity burdened his decision with an irresistible weight. Only a book like *L'Action* or one conceived in the same spirit could serve the goal Blondel had set himself.

Here, however, is the sensitive point where difficulties became knotty. Blondel did not want a simply juxtaposed philosophy and theology. He always reproached Scholasticism precisely for being content with such a position. "For Scholasticism," he used to say, "two subordinated orders in an ascendant hierarchy are superposed touching each other and communicating, but remaining external to one another." I do not know whether upon reading these lines Georges Perrot wondered how two orders could remain external one to the other, all the while communicating. All criticism would be sterile, because it would come down to reproaching Blondel for what was the very heart of his project: to establish the necessity of transcendence by a "method of immanence"; to analyze the general fact of action in order to detect an imbalance between "what we seem to think and will and do with what we really do, will, and think." This inner gap is the sign itself of the presence of the concept of transcendence, of the absence of the transcendent itself, but also of our disposition to receive it.

Why not take the risk? It was entirely legitimate on the condition, however, of not considering oneself the first to try it. It is to justify himself on this point that Blondel immediately rejected Scholasticism as a failed attempt, although he evidently knew almost nothing of it. What would he have thought if he had really known the immense perspective opened by Thomism, where all nature is there within the sight of grace and completely penetrated by it to its heart? Reading Blondel's irate denunciation of *extrinsicism* and *monophorism* in his 1904 articles on "History and Dogma," one feels as though one were dreaming, as if there had never been any Christian doctrine to conceive revelation, grace, in short the gift of God himself, like the gush of a stream in just one direction, a gift bestowed with nothing returning to the giver.

Two confusions muddle the discussion here, about at least the first of which Maurice Blondel appeared to have no doubts. He spoke about philosophy, while the problem he wanted to resolve by a philosophical method refers to the transcendent, which by definition comes under the jurisdiction of theology. Blondel wanted to establish by philosophical means that humans aspire to a supernatural goal. He thus wanted to establish a theological conclusion by philosophical means. Nothing shows better into what oblivion the concept of theology had fallen than this ceaselessly reaffirmed project of justifying by philosophical reason alone the affirmation of a supernatural order that, Blondel well knew, reason could never grasp nor even establish. His essentially contradictory undertaking was to legitimate a theology by appeal to the resources of philosophy alone. Without suspecting it, Blondel wanted to redo in *L'Action* the famed book III of the *Summa Contra Gentiles*. The problem posed is the same: why do beings act?

Chapter 19 replies: because all things want to assimilate themselves to God. Only, in St. Thomas, this is reason's answer to a theological problem. Thomas would not have maintained this thesis before a tribunal comprised of masters of the Arts Faculty. At least he would not have done so without warning them that he intended to speak to them as a theologian.

A second confusion follows from this point. Blondel judges Thomistic Scholasticism as if he were dealing with a philosophy of the kind he proposed to develop. His summary description of Scholasticism shows amazement that it is composed of two superposed orders in an *ascendant* hierarchy that touch each other and communicate, all the while "remaining external one to the other." This is how a philosopher sees theology, although in fact, for a theologian, we are dealing with a *descendent* hierarchy where everything comes from God before being able to rise back toward God. This is the very knot of the misunderstanding, from which the others stem and to which everything comes back. For, there is certainly a first extrinsicism, cause and end of all possible intrinsicisms. In the creative act, without which no problem can be posed, what is the creature's contribution? If monophorism is manifest anywhere, it is precisely where the creator makes being spring forth *ex nihilo creaturae*. The consequences of this initial fact have repercussions upon every aspect of the relation of humans to God. By whatever way humans go to their creator, the creator first must create them, call them, raise them up to him in order for them to go. The slightest knowledge of a theologian's theology and not of an amateur theology like that of philosophers, would have revealed to Maurice Blondel the inversion he made the problem's data undergo by making his method philosophical. There is a sorrowful distress of someone lost, alone with no fellow traveler, on the page of his *Itinéraire philosophique* where Blondel sees himself obligated to transpose all that he had found in his masters into a perspective "where it seemed that no one had methodically situated and maintained himself." He transposes what he found "even in St. Augustine," what he had "ended by discovering it in Spinoza, where Delbos had led him as to a secret rooftop terrace," what he found "even in my dear Pascal," he would add, "whom I did not excuse his not having searched for why we are embarked...." What an astonishing declaration! Here is a Christian who is presented as a rediscoverer of the Tradition and who neglects it to the point of believing himself called after twenty centuries of Christianity to resolve a problem vital to the Christian religion better than Augustine did, who furthermore is belatedly summoned. Blaise Pascal knew this tradition better, because he at least knew why we are embarked. But it is still a case of extrincisist monophorism. We are embarked because God embarked us, and he embarked us because he "first loved us." This is moreover in the first letter of John 4:10: "not our love for God, but God's love for us when he sent his Son," and further in 4:19, we see clearly where the human response is situated: "We are to love then, because he loved us first."

The sequel of Blondel's experiment is known. For a long time this great, even exemplary Christian was disturbed by feeling himself surrounded by a distrust whose cause remained invisible to him. Then he revisited the whole problem from the start, at least as much as a new philosophical beginning is possible on the threshold of old age. In 1934, forty-one years after the first edition of *L'Action*, the two volumes of *La Pensée* appeared; in 1935, *L'être et les êtres*, a "concrete and integral essay in ontology;" in 1936 *L'Action* was rewritten in two volumes, so profoundly changed that many found themselves immediately in search of the first, re-published for them in 1950. Last came several volumes devoted to the relations between philosophy and Christian spirit, where he was careful to preserve his beloved doctrinal solitude, about which he complained without being able to dispense with it. He continued to create fictional adversaries to have the pleasure of overcoming them. If we ask today what emerges from this effort, equal in length and passion, it is difficult to reply. Some of his interpreters want to see the essence of his doctrine in the first *L'Action*. Others, by contrast, place it in the last and furthermore unfinished tetralogy, while some scandalized observers bitterly reproach him for having betrayed his first philosophy by elaborating the second. The sad final eclipse of the warm friendship that had at first bound him to Fr. Laberthonnière painfully symbolizes the functional ambiguity in Maurice Blondel's thought. Was it really necessary to set aside great and authentic theologies with the sole result of creating so much disorder in many minds? As I have said, the man himself is above all praise, but the heir to Joseph Gratry by way of Léon Ollé-Laprune has yielded to the message of philosophism of method, though there was no trace of it in his heart.

There still remain Blondelians, but the school no longer gains recruits. Young Christians in search of a philosophy turn rather toward the work of Fr. Pierre Teilhard de Chardin than toward this convoluted dialectic, difficult to follow, whose word choice and sentence structure reflects its indecision in thought. Adorned with the prestige of science and served by the writer's style, of a poet, this new doctrine has just captured the attention of a vast public, as it merged from several years of subterranean life. Yesterday a professor was still asked: tell us about Blondel. Today, he is asked rather: tell us about Teilhard de Chardin.

The stunning success of Teilhard's doctrine would be inexplicable if he had nothing to say worth the trouble of being understood. It was even necessary, for his message to have been heard by a vast public, for his writings to know such circulation, that his thought should be scrutinized attentively, almost religiously by minds of the first order and that a veritable library of books devoted to his work, to his person even, should be published in our time. Many other things could be said in honor of the priest, the man, and the scientist, but none of that concerns the problem I have posed. I simply ask whether, after wanting to replace Thomism by Blondelism in teaching Christian theology, masters and students today will have to enlist in Teilhard de Chardin's school.

I would like to explain my reasons to doubt it and that firstly the prestige of the science by which his work is commended does not justify the theological authority that some desire to attribute to it. If there is an undeniable fact, it is that the only objectively demonstrable knowledge, scientific knowledge, is also the one that we can predict with certainty will cease to be true after a fairly short time. Science's very progress condemns it to devaluing itself continually. Descartes replaced Aristotle, but Newton replaced Descartes, as Einstein replaced Newton, without our being able to say with certainty what scientific universe will replace the one in which we live. The great scientific truth by which Fr. Teilhard de Chardin's thought is nourished is evolution. It has always been known that there was change. Today it is known that change extends to domains from which it was formerly excluded, for example that of heavenly bodies, but it is still not known either if this change follows a regular and constant path or how it is produced, or to what end, if there is one. Biologists sometimes put the reality of an evolution popularly understood in doubt and do so for purely scientific reasons. Theologians and metaphysicians have learned to remain in contact with science without claiming to interfere in its affairs for which they lack technical competence. It can only be said that founding a new theology upon the scientific concept of evolution would be to base oneself on a foundation whose solidity remains doubtful and whose meaning, in any case, is unclear.

So, the value and scientific meaning of this concept do not fall under our competence, but the theological use to which Fr. Teilhard de Chardin put it cannot help but catch the theologian's attention. For Thomists, in whose name I am supposed to speak, a first observation is inevitable: the apparently complete lack of knowledge of St. Thomas's doctrine that this scientist demonstrates. As a scientist that is his own concern, but insofar as he theologizes, the problem is different. I do not know what doctrine his professors taught him during his three years of philosophy at St. Louis House (Jersey, 1902–1905), followed then by his five years of theology at Ore Place (Sussex, 1908–1912), but I acknowledge that it would be somewhat impudent to deny him the stature of a competent theologian. My observation is much simpler and, I confess, almost incredibly naive. I am astonished that a priest, a religious, a member of the Society of Jesus whose fidelity to the directives of the Holy See is, so to speak, coessential to it, could invent, construct, and totally elaborate a Christian theology without giving the slightest attention that I know of, to the theology of the Church's Common Doctor.

I write these lines, I pronounce these words, without much hope of being believed. It is a matter of indifference to me that Fr. Teilhard de Chardin should have taught one theology or another. I have neither the competence to judge it nor authority to intervene. I do not reproach Fr. Teilhard de Chardin for anything, particularly for not being a Thomist, because I am not sure that he could have become one even if he had tried. What astounds me is that after nine years of studies in the course of which he must have heard the doctrine discussed and knowing that others still take it seriously, study it, are nourished by it, not a word from him lets us guess how he himself understood it. Nor are we told why he believed himself excused from taking it into account, and integrating his own Christology into something that our common Church, which was his as it was ours, recommends to our respectful attention. I am concerned not with his person but with the situation itself and its paradoxical possibility, for we all suffer its repercussions. Unless still unpublished documents some day explain it to us, it is impossible for those who identify with Thomistic theology to know why—ignorance, misunderstanding, or well-grounded opposition—Fr. Teilhard de Chardin believed himself entitled to theologize without mentioning it.

Therefore, it remains for us to do our best and assume our responsibilities to say what we think of his doctrine, I repeat, insofar as teachable in schools in place of St. Thomas Aquinas's doctrine.

We cannot be Thomists without being ready to accept unreservedly every demonstrated scientific conclusion. We ought to take as a model in this regard the late Fr. Antonin Sertillanges, O.P., the theologian most intelligently open to the discoveries of science that I have known. Like St. Thomas, he did not accept scientific truth because he had to do so, but from the bottom of his heart, and he loved God in it. Many proofs of this could be cited, if this were the place. Fr. Teilhard de Chardin's personal contribution, particularly in the realm of paleontology, falls under the history of science only, but one cannot read his theological speculation without immediately seeing that it lacks any specifically scientific justification. We could distinguish the mineral, vegetable, animal, and human kingdoms without him. Bergson would suffice without him to penetrate and animate these four kingdoms with a continual stream of creative evolution, but when Teilhard invites us to organize this scientific view of the universe around the person of Christ, even without wondering what the historical Christ becomes in the new functions with which he is charged, one hesitates greatly to follow the theologian's imagination in the poetical world to which he introduces us. Anyone who has followed the history of Christian thought finds himself in familiar territory. Theilhardian theology is one more Christian gnosis and like every gnosis from Marcion to our day, it is *theology fiction*. All the traditional marks of the genre are found here: a cosmic perspective on all problems or perhaps rather a cosmogenetic perspective, a cosmogenetic morality, a cosmogenetic vision. We have a cosmic matter, a cosmic Christ, and since he is the physical center of creation, we have a Christ who is essentially "evolver," humanizer, in short a "universal Christ," in as much as the Incarnation is the explanation of the universal mystery. In this way, the cosmogenesis becomes Christogenesis, creative of the Christic and the Christosphere, the order that crowns the noosphere and perfects it through the transforming presence of Christ. This fine vocabulary is not cited as wrong in itself, but merely as symptomatic of the taste that every gnosis evinces for moving neologisms, suggesting unfathomable perspectives weighted with affectivity.

Once again, Teilhardism is not being accused here, and it will not be judged. We simply want to know why this vision, born in the mind of a scientist priest endowed with a powerful poetic imagination, ought to be taught in our schools as a faithful expression of the teaching of the Church and of the Christian faith. Though all are free to immerse themselves in the mysteries of the pleroma and pleromaization, it is necessary to remember that concepts of this kind are not guaranteed by any scientific view of the world and humanity, evolutionary or not. We should also recall that this whole pseudoscientific scheme does not even have the merit of being accepted by everyone nowadays, as Aristotelianism was in the thirteenth century. Finally, if we succeed in permeating the young minds entrusted to our professors with Teilhardism, everyone can have the certainty of seeing their theology go out of fashion soon and the system collapse in their minds along with the world order that provisionally sustained it. Perhaps it would not misrepresent the doctrine to say that it tries to translate Christian teaching into the language of an integrally evolutionary vision of nature. One can imagine Christian scientists who enjoy having their Christian faith expressed in a language familiar to them, and all are free to attempt this adventure on their own, but to arbitrarily engage others in it can hardly be excused.

Besides, some people would oblige us to follow not Teilhard de Chardin today, but rather Martin Heidegger, the Freiburg philosopher whose hermetic language is so seductive for many that it is enough for them to have learned to speak it to be persuaded that they have understood him.

From the standpoint of our problem, Heidegger is no different from Blondel and Teilhard de Chardin. For Heidegger, Thomism is the symbol of an unknown reality. What St. Thomas said about existence seems not to be known to him. If he knew it, it is surprising that he should say nothing about it in moments when his personal set of problems makes it almost a duty to speak of Thomas. However, in our times, it is a badge of honor to feel that when one listens to Heidegger philosophy speaks through this strange voice, and perhaps neo-Scholastics have felt this more vividly than others. In the measure in which the obscure words of the master become more intelligible to them, they recognize in it old truths that they possessed themselves as their inheritance, but that they chalked up to Heidegger's credit in the joy of acknowledging them. The same panic that pushes the wealthy to covet the poor man's hut if it is new has thrust certain of our Thomists onto the trail of this profound but obscure thinker. They hope he will guide them to where they have never been. In fact it is he who has not yet ever gone where they have been for a long time.

A theologian recently said that it is evident "that Heidegger's thought cannot be compared or assimilated to Scholastic thought in general and to St. Thomas's philosophy in particular without mutual harm." I do not know what will happen to Scholasticism because of this comparison, but perhaps it has become inevitable, since Heidegger has confronted Thomist Scholasticism in a proposition that Thomism's mere existence invites us to regard as inexact: "Insofar as metaphysics only puts forward being *qua* being, it does not think about existence itself."[1] And a little before in the same *Return to the Foundation of Metaphysics*[2] Heidegger was already saying: "Because metaphysics examines being as being, it restricts itself to the being and does not turn to existence as existence." On account of that, continues Heidegger, metaphysics is insufficient for one who wants to think about existence.

Heidegger has no luck with the Middle Ages. When he thought he was dealing with Duns Scotus, he was in contact with Thomas of Erfurt, which is unimportant, but here, it must be said, the mistake is more serious, because it is a fault of omission. For Heidegger metaphysics is that of Aristotle, and Brentano taught him that the Philosopher's metaphysics concerns being as being. However, Brentano himself was ignorant of the existence of another metaphysics, that of St. Thomas, which also concerns being as being but additionally proposes to push into the heart of being, to existence, Brentano did not teach Heidegger about that other metaphysics. Thomism

1   [Translator: English has difficulty expressing a distinction that French, German, and Latin can make between being in the sense of a thing and being in the sense of something's existing. Normal French (or Spanish) would probably also use the same word for both, except that it would be the infinitive instead of the participle, but they do have a technical philosophical term for being-thing. To retain the flavor of what was originally a spoken lecture, the English existence seemed best for Latin *esse* or French *être* (as opposed to *étant*). This is not uncontroversial.]

2   [Translator: The reference seems to be to *Le retour au fondement de la métaphysique* translated by Roger Munier, one of the short writings included in Martin Heidegger, *Questions ... Qu'est-ce que la métaphysique?, Ce que fait l'être-essential d'un fondement ou raison, De l'Essence de la vérité, Contribution à la question de l'être, Identité et différence*, trans. Henry Corbin, Roger Munier, Alphonse de Waelhens, Walter Biemel, Paris: Galimard, 1968, pp. 315.]

is a philosophy of *Sein* insofar as it is a philosophy of *esse*. When young people invite us to discover Martin Heidegger, they invite us to rediscover St. Thomas Aquinas's trans-ontic metaphysics without knowing it. This is all we can say on this subject. It would be interesting to know what Heidegger would have thought if he had known of the existence of a metaphysics of *esse*, before taking his own initial decisions. But it will never be known. It is too late. What we point out to vindicate ourselves against an unforeseen objection is specifically different from what we would have thought had we foreseen it. *Nachdenken* is not *denken*. Happily, we are not responsible for resolving the unsolvable problem: what would have happened if Heidegger had known of the existence of this metaphysics that does completely the contrary of what metaphysics always does according to him? What might this doctrine signify for him, which *weil sie das Seiende als Seiende befragt, bleibt nich beim Seienden und kehrt sich stets an das Sein als Sein*? How could we know, since Heidegger himself will never know? I only pose the question in order to suggest to those who hurry to pursue it that there is no risk in delay. Perhaps we have only a delay in our advance. We are in a hurry to follow those whom we have left behind.

Taking another look at those more or less serious crises, the most recent of which is never the last, it seems to me that they all have at least one point in common, which is the fear of being left behind by progress and of missing the truth. The Thomist's crime is to be a traditionalist, a stick-in-the-mud, blind to new views that the Spirit never ceases to discover.

No doubt there is some truth in this reproach, because it is always difficult to renounce a past that one knows and loves. For one like me, who has so slowly won a partial understanding of the truth that is destined to remain partial, if I had to renounce that truth whose meditation is a constant joy for me for a higher truth, I would do so with regret. Still, I would do so, if it were necessary, to remain faithful to at least the spirit of the doctrine. By contrast, I wonder at the fatuousness of those who, knowing nothing of the past, pride themselves on leaving it behind. Since nothing holds them back, they unceasingly hurl themselves forward, advancing like Panurge's sheep that nothing could stop on the road of progress. The real revolutionary, on the contrary, is the person who holds a truth firmly, however old as it may be, though the whole world abandons it. Those who reproach him for his error will one day perhaps be happy to accept it as tomorrow's truth.

Part II:
Three Essays: On Teilhard, Marxism, and Vatican II

IV
The Teilhard de Chardin Case[1]

I have taken no part in any of the controversies that have developed around the work and memory of Fr. Pierre Teilhard de Chardin. Once, recently, I had to express an opinion because my subject required it. Invited to say what I think of the doctrine, I resign myself to do so reluctantly. I would even have refused, had it not seemed to me that I would have the occasion here to say certain useful things, although it would perhaps be more prudent to be silent. Following an American journalistic approach that I find excellent, I will begin by saying in a few lines what I propose to develop in this article, which will dispense busy people from reading it.

Fr. Teilhard de Chardin's thought does not seem to me to have ever attained the minimum degree of consistency required to be able to speak of a *doctrine* in this connection. This is why I will only speak of the Teilhard de Chardin case. Likewise, although Teilhard's manner of thinking is completely foreign to me, not to say something stronger, I think that those who hope for an official censure of it are mistaken about what they disapprove of. A doctrine that does not exist cannot be censured.

* * *

I never followed Fr. Teilhard de Chardin's scientific-theological output. The bulk of his writings was not published during his lifetime. He himself

1   I feel unable to shy away from an invitation to examine Fr. Teilhard de Chardin's position in itself and now not as a possible substitute for St. Thomas's theology to be taught in Catholic schools, all the more because it gives me the opportunity to develop the previous lecture's overly brief explanation regarding Fr. Teilhard's attitude. We are not dealing with a fourth lecture but a written supplement to the third. This chapter was never given as a lecture.

never personally sent me a single one of them, and none came to me through an intermediary. So I did not have the honor of being one of his friends, but I encountered him twice in unforgettable circumstances. I believe that his friends will understand me when I say that were it only for the beauty of his face, the charm of his voice, and the aristocratic distinction of his whole personality, I am very happy to have known him.

The first time was in the home of close common friends. I had the honor of attending the baptism of a newborn in the capacity of godfather. The priest was Fr. Teilhard de Chardin. I was immediately captivated by this scion of aristocratic stock. If I may say so, he baptized the infant with us; I mean that we baptized him together. Father involved us in the rite, commenting on it as he went, explaining it, and taking us into his confidence. I have never doubted that Fr. Teilhard de Chardin honored the priesthood, but if the temptation had come to me, the memory of that christening would have nipped the evil thought in the bud. I hold his person in unreserved esteem and profound respect.

The second encounter was totally different, and without negating the first, it has continued to perplex me. It took place in 1954 during a symposium organized by Columbia University. We gathered for several days at Arden House near New York. He and I met at the moment of our arrival. As soon as he spotted me, he came to meet me, his face glowing with an open smile and placing both hands on my arms said, "Can you tell me who will finally give us that meta-Christianity that we are all waiting for?"

I hesitated for a long time to report the phrase. It seemed implausible coming from a priest. Besides, to my knowledge, if he penned similar things, he still did not write that. I make it public today, because re-reading his writings with the occasion of this essay, I think I have finally understood. Later I will say how I interpret the expression, and why my recollection seems plausible now. At the time, however, this abrupt approach to the subject left me disconcerted. I think I stammered a few confused words such as that Christianity was already a great deal for me and that I was waiting to see it through in order to try to go beyond it. Father saw clearly that I was not in orbit and had the charity to change the subject. His antennae were sensitive enough to feel my awkwardness, and the subject was never raised again between us.

But the same day in the course of the afternoon, in a passageway traversed by a continuous throng of people, I passed by a priest seated in an armchair totally unaware of what was going on around him and absorbed in reading his breviary. It was Fr. Teilhard de Chardin of the Society of Jesus. These two images sum up for me what I call the Teilhard de Chardin case. Even if he really awaited a "meta-Christianity," it is in Christianity that he had already found it.

* * *

Subsequently, I have often thought about this encounter, all the more because Father Teilhard's extraordinary posthumous celebrity recalled it. Books by him were published, and I tried to read them, unsuccessfully I must confess, and I acknowledge that this lack of sympathy for the author's intellectual style disqualifies me from speaking about him. I have a dread of imprecision and fuzziness in intellectual knowledge. As much as I enjoy them in poetry where they have full citizenship, they are unbearable to me in disciplines like science that can be difficult but not vague, or in theology, which is the most exact of the sciences dealing with a real object, whatever those who have not practiced it may say. St. Augustine recalled: *nobis ad certam regulam loqui fas est.*

I am far from having a balance sheet on Teilhard de Chardin. I admit lack of patience with a writer when his language is burdened with neologisms that neither necessity nor meaning obviously require. I always mistrust writers who use capitals. Capitals are normal in German where they mean nothing; they are not in French, where they ought to mean something if they are used. A capital adds nothing to a word's meaning. *Life, Evolution, Reflection, Death,* and so forth, mean no more than life, evolution, reflection, or death. What does using this artifice try to tell me? Does the author want to condition me, as they say nowadays, or does he really think that words written in this way get a deeper meaning than ordinarily? I do not know, but, since in any case the supplementary meaning eludes me, I am uneasy. I even have the vague impassion of a kind of injustice toward me. Who is this scientist who does not speak the language of science? Who is this theologian who does not speak the language of theology? In either case, he is not situated in the line of his predecessors the continuation of whose labor is the issue at hand. He is neither Thomas Aquinas nor Albert the Great in theology, not Einstein nor Newton in physics. Rather I get the impression that Teilhard de Chardin has embarked on a completely personal spiritual adventure, and wants to enlist me, even if for that I must give up my own quest supported by the dual religious and philosophical tradition in which I have been raised. I certainly know that this tradition seems outdated to him, but one cannot practice it for a long time without wondering what he knew about it himself. I know nothing about the answer that would be appropriate for this question. Enough then of rash suppositions, and let us rather attempt to bring out the main outlines of what he wanted to be, inspiring ourselves by what he has been.

* * *

He wanted to be a priest early. He was one, and he was even an irreproachable Jesuit, one could say a model, thinking about the difficult situation in which he found himself. He also wanted to be a competent naturalist, a paleontologist more precisely, because mankind was at the center of his interest. But if he had only been that, his work would interest few people today, beyond his friends, his confreres, and some specialists. There have been many Jesuit scientists from the seventeenth century to our time, and we are happy to honor the memory of those who are still known. The celebrity that Fr. Teilhard de Chardin's work enjoys does not have questionable origins. Everything here is pure. Nothing in this activity pays court to the elemental instincts than contemporary publicity exploits for its advantage. Even his immense love for matter is completely spiritual, because he loves its weight, texture, structure, and color, in short that bouquet of savory sensible qualities that led certain ancients to say that matter is the intelligible coagulated in some manner. Far from criticizing him for some obscure tendency toward materialism, in him we rather taste a beneficent recalling of God's presence in his work. Teilhard de Chardin loves the traces, the vestiges in matter of its creator. One would say, a Christian Gaston Bachelard.

However, it is not to the scientist that his opus owes its prestige. Few of those who admire it have read "The Mammals of the Lower French Eocene and Their Deposits." The works called scientific to which he owes his fame are vast frescoes painted by a vigorous imagination which in no way resembles the slow, patient summations of scientists like Fr. Breuil, for instance, which do not lack imagination (How could one be a scientist without it?), but which only commit to paper the results of verified observations. Even an essentially philosophical work like Bergson's *Creative Evolution* published in 1907 has superlative scientific rigor compared to "The Cosmic Life" (1916), "My Universe" (1918), or "Christ the Evolver" (1941).[2] A scientist can expand his ambition even to wanting to describe the universe, although ordinarily other scientists raise their eyebrows at the mere pretense of this, but if he announces his intention to describe *his* universe, everyone will immediately know that we are no longer dealing with science. The result of such an endeavor immediately is placed in a well known and certainly quite noble genre, but one where so many *Ages of the World* and *Tableaus of Nature* were already accumulated in the past, which make more of a mark in the history of letters than of science. Fr. Teilhard de Chardin scientist is not at issue, and we know he enjoyed the respect of his peers. The only thing I recall here is the author of what is very appropriately called *Versuch einer Weltsumme*, because it is also the only one whose production has won the hearing of a mass public, and I only say that the project of establishing a summa of the universe is not a scientific proposition. What enjoys the prestige of science in Teilhard de Chardin's output is not the output of the true scientist that he was.

* * *

Moreover, the best among the numerous studies devoted to Teilhard's work are not misled on this point. It is enough to see their titles to observe that they do not set forth his strictly scientific side: *La pensée théologique de Teilhard de Chardin* by Georges Crespy (1961), *La pensée religieuse du Père Teilhard de Chardin* by his confrere and friend Fr. Henri de Lubac (1962), *Bergson et Teilhard de Chardin* by Madeleine Barthélmey-Madoule (1963). These titles make it rather clear where the attention of his friends, admirers, and disciples is directed. The philosopher and the theologian interest them primarily. But was he a philosopher? And if he was a theologian, in what sense was he?

One hardly dares to set out in this area, because it is rather a quagmire.

2   [Translator] "La vie cosmic" and "Mon univers" are included in *Writings in the Time of War*, trans. René Hague, London: Collins, 1968. "Christ evoluteur" is included in *Christianity and Evolution*, trans. René Hague, San Diego, Harcourt, 1971.

No universally admitted definition of philosopher or theologian exists, other than that the former attempts to study wisdom and the latter speaks about God, but there are a thousand ways of doing both, and nobody has the right to reject ways different from his own. Therefore, I will say first that I do not refuse Fr. Teilhard de Chardin either of these titles. I would only like to compare his way of possessing them with that of some others. Accordingly, being incapable of choosing, I will ask one of his most faithful interpreters which concept he would himself situate at the heart of this view of the world.

"That man as key to the universe," we are told, "is one of the greatest affirmation of Teilhard's thought."[3] This is completely true. However, it is at odds with the first question: are we in science or in philosophy? No doubt it will be answered that Teilhardism's peculiarity is to be a unitary view and that these artificial distinctions lack interest. Perhaps for Teilhard and for his admirers, but for others these distinctions subsist, and they are particularly relevant to our not being made to believe that we are still in science when we are already in philosophy or theology. Propositions do not have the same value of certainty in the three orders. The three orders are not even knowledge of the same kind. One sometimes wonders whether what Fr. Teilhard de Chardin imagines fits into any known kind of knowledge.

The specific character of his thought is to have shed light on the peculiar and eminent place of man in the panorama of evolution. This concept used to be regarded as a stale theological claim. The universe was made for man; this naive anthromorphism was mocked. That universal evolution leads to man as its summit seems new. Let us admit it, since we have read somewhere that the world was not made in a day, but that the mineral kingdom preceded and prepared for the vegetable kingdom, which made the

3   Claude Cuénot, *Teilhard de Chardin*, Paris: Éditions du Seuil, 1963, p. 94. This excellent introduction to a subject its author knows better than anyone else will be of the greatest utility. Cuénot is a convinced Teilhardian, even a little touchy. He classifies books on Teilhard not be their intrinsic value but by their degree of sympathy for the doctrine: "masterpiece of idiocy and malevolence," "very reticent," "more open," "traditionalist who tries to be open," etc. Salvation is hardly to be hoped for a mind that, thinking differently from Father, cannot honestly give allegiance.

animal kingdom possible, whose king was Adam, the last to appear on the scene. Certain paleontologists seem to have seen an important discovery there. It would not be the first time that revelation opened unexpected perspectives of intelligibility to reasons whose view is blocked by facts. If we judge by the little part of the physical universe that can be seen from earth, it is in a way immediately, intuitively, evident that man is the image of God through knowledge and the end and glory of creation. But this is not science. Pascal was rather amused by that candle that took itself to be the goal of creation. Since Pascal and Voltaire agree for once, we must suspect the presence of a truth in their words.

Teilhard de Chardin remains unshakably faithful to the truth of scriptural tradition, but in him it becomes a kind of rational certainty whose nature is not evident. Having recalled that his thought was always as sensitive to discontinuity as to continuity, the same privileged interpreter adds that, by that very fact, "the human phenomenon not only presents great novelty, a great extension, but appears as the end of an operation that seems to be connected with the deepest history of the whole world. In optimal conditions, matter spontaneously tends to become vitalized. In the same conditions life tends to be hominized. The noosphere prolongs the biosphere. Noogenesis or birth of reflected intelligence (we could equally well speak of anthropogenesis in the birth of man) is aligned with biogenesis."[4] It would not be an exaggeration to say that Teilhard de Chardin's human, an exceptional being, is the key to many things. He is the key to universal evolution.

But who is speaking here? What is this kind of reasoning or thought, and what is the issue? When it is said that matter that tends to be vitalized when conditions are favorable, or that life tends to be hominized "in the same conditions," does this not mean that things happen when the required conditions came together? It seems that we are pleased to imagine that the causes that this has happened are known. It certainly is necessary that they should have been present, because their effects were ultimately produced. In fact, with this science or philosophy we are not so far from the time when opium made someone sleep because it had a dormitive virtue whose effect was to make the senses drowsy. Why does life appear? Because the moment of its appearing

4   Cuénot, *Teilhard*, p. 93.

came.[5] Fr. Teilhard, who is a contemplative, does not cease to admire the world, and it is the world itself that he puts forward as its own explanation.

* * *

If this is neither science nor philosophy, will it not be theology? The question is all the more legitimate since, when his adversaries attack him in this field, his defenders immediately devote themselves to proving that in reality all these grand intuitions are of Christian origin.

I think they are right, and if I were a non-believing scientist reading Teilhard de Chardin for the first time, I believe I would not let myself be caught by the pseudo-scientific wrapping in which this Jesuit cloaks his view of the world. In all his chapters, old Christian ideas are encountered under a language that is not even always new. I have already recalled the formation of the world by stages according to the Biblical narrative that St. Augustine deemed more philosophical to not take literally.[6] In Fr. Teilhard

5   Claude Cuénot's exposition necessarily simplifies the doctrine, but it does not betray it. By way of example, here is what Teilhard himself affirms "on positively verifiable reasons," Teilhard assures: "What explains the biological revolution caused by the apparition of Man is an explosion of consciousness, and what in turn explains this explosion of consciousness is just simply [!] the passage of a privileged line of *corpusculization*, that is to say a zoological phylum, through the previously impenetrable surface that separated the zone of direct Pyschism from that of reflected Psychism. Having arrived at a critical point of arrangement following this particular line (or as we say here, of winding up), life is hypercentered on itself to the point of becoming capable of foresight and discovery." Pierre Teilhard de Chardin, *Le group zoologique humain, Structure et directions évolutives*, preface by Jean Piveteau, Paris: Éditions Albin Michel, 1956, p. 79. Where should what the author himself calls "reconstructions of the Past" be classified? He objects to the fatality that makes their beginnings casually disappear (Teilhard, *Le groupe zoologique*, pp. 30, 43, 81–82). In what concerns the point of departure of Anthropogenesis, this is what Fr. Teilhard styles "finding a serious *blank space* in our representation of the Past" (p. 82). In these conditions, the history of the origins of man offers the same certainty as the origins of society in Rousseau's *Social Contract*. But Rousseau does not think he is doing science. On the contrary, he denies it expressly.

6   St. Augustine, a refined philosophical mind, interprets the genesis narrative metaphorically. He judges that the works of the "six days" was really the work of a moment. God created the world "in a blink of the eye." As his scripture

everything takes place as if nature produces everything from itself for humans and humans for God. This God is the Alpha and the Omega. The Cosmic Christ is the first born of creation. These and many other similar traits tempt readers to think that they are witnessing a Christian transposition of science's cosmogenesis rather than the contrary.

Regarding constant ambiguity, I speak not of Fr. Teilhard's thought but of his writings. Let us not expect that theologians will ever resign themselves to tolerating this method because it is the contrary of their own. While scientists will suspect him of conducting a disguised apologetical undertaking, because there is too much of St. Paul in him, theologians will complain that this St. Paul completely becomes Teilhard there. They will both be right, and it is there that we find the heart of the problem, in my opinion, because what is specific to his endeavor finally lets itself be detected.

Science, philosophy, and theology are given together in his work because they are so already in the author's person. All of St. Paul becomes Teilhard passing through him, because the Teilhard ingredient includes intact and miraculously preserved, as it were under continual scientific or other alluviums the pure gold nugget of childhood piety and faith. He himself underlined this continuity, which is an essential element to comprehending his writings. The Cosmic Christ was first Baby Jesus for him, and he must always remain that. The newborn of Christmas is exactly the same as the one who became "the child of Bethlehem and the Crucified one, the Prime Mover and the world itself's collector Nucleus."[7]

text Augustine has "creavit omnia simul (Ecclesiasticus 18:1). Commenting on this text in the *Summa Theologiae*, part I, question 74, article 2 reply to objection 2, St. Thomas concludes, "quod Deus creavit omnia simul quantum ad rerum substantiam quodammodo informem; sed quantum ad formationem, quae facta est per distinctionem et ornatum non simul; unde signanter utitur verbo creationis." If we wanted to play this game, we might wonder which of these two doctrines would enjoy the favor of a modern partisan of evolution.

7 Quoted by Claude Cuénot, *Teilhard*, p. 65. Perhaps the end of the passage needs to be quoted: "this God [no longer only of the old Cosmos but of the new Cosmogenesis] ... this God so much awaited by our generation, is it not exactly you Jesus, who represent him, and who bring him to us?" The God awaited by the new generation is certainly the Christ of Bethlehem in development, "Christ always greater."

Many read Teilhard de Chardin, and he nourishes their reflections. Some, no doubt, benefit, but is his personal experience transferable? Some may imagine that it is transferable, because the quasi-magic words that envelop his thoughts can be learned and repeated. There is a Teilhardian terminology that lets everybody speak of Baby Jesus as identical to the Nuclear-Collector-of-the-world-unto-itself, but in how many souls is this love of Baby Jesus, to which Teilhard never ceases to refer as the ever burning hearth of his inner life, even on the threshold of old age as it was in Teilhard de Chardin's soul?

And yet, but for that his doctrine no longer has any meaning. One had to be Teilhard in order to keep this "God finished for himself, and however, for us never finished being born, present in thought to the end," this God as he calls him "evoluter and evolutive," and to be able to say to him other than as a rhetorical device: "Lord of my childhood and Lord of my end." Who else but Teilhard can claim, like him, to place this same Baby Jesus, that we learned to know and love at our mother's knee, "at the heart of universal matter." Teilhard's readers may well get the letter of his cosmic vision from him, the ideas and concepts into which his thought is translated. They cannot get his own religious experience from him, his faith so simple, so pure that nothing ever shook, and which is essential to the meaning of his work. To believe oneself capable of living Fr. Teilhard de Chardin's thought, it is necessary not to be a mediocre Christian. In all sincerity, I do not think the thought is dangerous, because I do not think it is transferable. But I cannot say that I take it to be true, because that is a whole other question.

* * *

Fr. Teilhard de Chardin enjoyed almost unbelievable fame certain of whose manifestations are not of a very good sort. One understands that *Planète* takes an interest in the apostle of planetization and the author of "The Phases of a Living Planet,"[8] but Teilhard is not responsible for his

8   [Translator: "A Great Event Foreshadowed: The Planetization of Mankind" (1945) was chapter VII and "From the Pre-Human to the Ultra-Human: the Phases of a Living Planet (1950) chapter XXII in *The Future of Man*, translated by Norman Denny, Harper and Row, 1959, Image Books/Random House, 2004.]

posthumous fame, he who sought it so little while living. And then, as Émile Faguet said one day, "Success proves nothing, not even against someone."

I must admit that the only thing that troubles me (I speak about the worth of his thought, not of his influence) is that being regarded as charged with a kind of doctrinal mission and specifically one of theological reform, he remained so badly informed about what he intended to replace by a renewed Christian wisdom. Like those explorers who know all countries except their own, Fr. Teilhard could tell the history of the world from the beginning, but neither the history of philosophy or theology was familiar to him. With several great Catholics of his time, Teilhard decreed that Scholastic theology was outdated without ever taking the trouble to draw up an objective balance sheet of it and submit it to serious critical examination. One is tired of hearing people who think they have critical minds reject Scholasticism in its totality as an abstract system of empty concepts or even, because they latch on there, as Latin "juridicism." None of them has wondered about the possible solution of the key problem that Scholasticism at least had the merit of defining and scrutinizing with indefatigable courage: what is the meaning of the word of God and to what point could our reason go before our faith?

His excellent biographer, whose fidelity to Fr. Teilhard is total to the point of sometimes being overly susceptible, says that, "the relations between the two halves of Pierre Teilhard's soul were difficult at first." Conflicts set "cosmic sense and Christian sense" in opposition. Between 1892 and 1897, again we are told, "the student of the Mongré School experienced some difficulty in reconciling his attraction for nature with the [very narrow] evangelism of the *Imitation of Christ*. Toward 1901–1902, the young seminarian went through a serious crisis. He seriously considered the possibility of completely abandoning the science of stones in order to devote himself entirely to supernatural activities. If he did not completely go off the rails at that point, he owed that to the robust good sense of Fr. Paul Troussard [Master of novices]."[9]

Fr. Troussard did what was necessary, because there appears to be no reason why a priest, even a religious, should not be a paleontologist. On

9   Claude Cuénot, *Teilhard*, p. 19.

the contrary, I would like someone to tell us some day why the calling of paleontologist or anthropologist is so often combined with that of priest. It only would have been necessary do two other things: persuade young Teilhard to engage himself fully in his theological studies, if he had competent professors to guide him, and above all to convince him that when someone has the privilege of doing scientific studies like those in which he was soon going to become a professor, one cannot be satisfied with dreaming about the nature of evolution. Rather it is necessary to measure it against established facts and clarify it in their light. I think that the scientific discussion of the concept of natural evolution by the evolutionists of the first half of the twentieth century does honor to the human mind. What was formed early in young Teilhard's thought, the same biographer says, and what opened up to him toward 1908–1912, was completely different in origin and nature: it was the "emergence in his mind of a synthesis, under great monistic pressure, between the cult of matter, the cult of life, and the cult of energy."[10] That makes a lot of cults. In the measure in which this language faithfully reproduces Fr. Teilhard's thought, it is difficult to find precise meaning. It is neither the language of a scientist nor of scientific thought. What is it then?

* * *

Sometimes I try to imagine the situation of a "definer," charged according to the well-established method, with extracting propositions from Fr. Teilhard's writings or with reducing the doctrine to them. Teilhard never ceased to say that he had no system, but it must be added that his thought does not consist of a linked series of propositions. All the propositions that one pleases to extract from his writings or to impute to him slip through the censor's fingers. Only thoughts can be criticized usefully, not expressions with indeterminate meaning. If there is a theology of Teilhard de Chardin, it is entirely different from what is given this label in the schools. He did not propose to make traditional theology progress or to rectify it on this or that point, but rather to carry out new theological work neglected by the old theology and which it is consequently useless to try to judge from the latter's viewpoint.

10   Claude Cuénot, *Teilhard*, p. 18.

The new task that he intended to take on, at least to set in motion, is perfectly defined in "Christianity and Evolution. Suggestions for a New Theology."[11] "Broadly, it can be said that if the general concern of theology during the Church's first centuries was to define intellectually and mystically the position of Christ in relation to the Trinity, in our days its vital interest has become the following: to analyze and specify the relations of existence and influence linking Christ and the universe to one another."[12]

I believe that no text from Fr. Teilhard is more significant or states the meaning of his undertaking more clearly and simply. For him, the issue is not to propose such or such a new theological thesis, but to displace the entire perspective of Christology. Old Christology (from the beginnings to the twentieth century) is Christ and the Trinity. New Christology, since around 1908–1912 is Christ and the Cosmos. Here the cosmic Christ takes precedence over the Trinitarian Christ. How do we want theologians for whom, since the first days of the Church, Christ is above all the Son, to transpose all of Teilhard de Chardin's cosmic problematic back into their own language? As a consequence, misunderstandings invariably abound. Teilhard denies nothing in traditional theology, on the contrary. But he wants the characteristics "imposed by tradition on the Word to get out of metaphysics and law and take their position realistically and without violence in the number of and at the head of the most fundamental currents that Science acknowledges in the Universe today."[13]

"Fabulous position," Fr. Teilhard adds, "it must be affirmed as Christ's." Assuredly, but also complete transposition of Christology. It would be a mistake to imagine that Fr. Teilhard is not completely aware of the nature of his undertaking. On the contrary, he knows that he is trying to effectuate a "generalization of Christ-Redeemer in a veritable Christ evolver."[14] It is true that St. Paul is not unaware of the cosmic meaning of the person of Christ, but if Christ-Redeemer is not in the forefront of his doctrine, then

11 [Translator: "Christianity and Evolution. Suggestions for a New Theology" is chapter XII of *Christianity and Evolution*, translated by René Hague, London: William Collins, 1969; and Harvest Books (Orlando, Florida: Harcourt Brace, 1974). "Christ the Evolver" is chapter X.
12 Claude Cuénot, *Teilhard*, p.141.
13 Claude Cuénot, *Teilhard*, p.141.
14 Claude Cuénot, *Teilhard*, p.142.

no one has ever understood him. Fr. Teilhard does not retreat from this hypothesis. Full of the grandeur and beauty of modern science, he sees himself called to accomplish a theological revolution by modern science, similar to the one that marked the opening of the Christian era. "In the Church's first century, Christianity made its definitive entrance into human thought by boldly assimilating Jesus of the Gospel to the Alexandrian Logos."[15] Today the issue is no longer to give Christ access to human thought but to maintain him there. That can only be if, by a decision as bold as the first, today's theology assimilates Christ to the cosmic force that is origin and goal of evolution. What a revolution! We are invited simply to bring back the faith in the Redeemer to its proper place.

* * *

It is useless to be indignant and superfluous to condemn. As I have said, Fr. Teilhard de Chardin's case is completely personal, but those who only see the outside can let themselves be seduced by the poetry with which his doctrine abounds. Moreover, there is good reason for this, because the spectacle of creation singing the Creator's glory has always been a source of inspiration for Christian thinkers. The scientific concept of universal evolution is fascinating and it is natural that it holds many minds in a kind of enchantment. This is no reason for us to renounce the exercise of our judgment and to seek, not what Fr. Teilhard de Chardin ought to have thought but what we ourselves ought to think of him.

First of all, Fr. Teilhard is mistaken about what happened in the second century A.D. He conceives this first reform as the model of what he wants to accomplish himself. The Apologetic Fathers did not boldly assimilate "Jesus of the Gospels to the Alexandrian Logos." It is completely the reverse. In a still much bolder endeavor, they assimilated the Alexandrian Logos to Christ the Savior of the Gospel. To the philosophers they offered the proposition, this time truly fabulous but Christian: that Logos about whom you talk so much, we know him because he was made flesh and loved among us. This incredible adventure befell the philosophers' Logos: it became Jesus of Nazareth. Those who do not understand the words of the first Christian masters, from St. Justin to Clement of Alexandria are mistaken about the

15   Claude Cuénot, *Teilhard*, p.142.

meaning of their writings. This is why Clement could have been called a "Christian Gnostic," because in him it is the faith itself that is true knowledge, true gnosis. What do they other Gnostics do? They indeed assimilate Jesus to the Logos; they cosmify Christ at the same time that they christify the universe. To make a second revolution today analogous to the first, it would be necessary to say with all possible force, not that Christ is Evolution, but that Evolution is Christ.[16]

The first shift of perspective brings with it a second, which is the substitution of science for faith, because the identification of religious belief with scientific knowledge amounts to suppressing the former. This identification becomes inevitable when the object of faith is that of science. The ambivalence of the concept of Christ in Teilhard de Chardin has just this origin. In one stroke he can speak of "this elevation of the historical Christ to a universal physical function" and of this "ultimate identification of Cosmogenesis with Christogenesis." Note the word *elevation*. We get the "neologos of modern philosophy" that is no longer the redeemer of Adam, but "the evolver principle of a universe in movement." We will be told: see how careful he is to preserve Christ. Yes, but what Christ? That of the gospel, or that of science? Now is the moment to recall the principle posited by St.

---

16 I have insisted as vigorously as I could about the meaning of the doctrine of the Word in the fourth gospel and in the first Christian thinkers in *History of Christian Philosophy in the Middle Ages*, New York: Random House, 1955, p. 6. The issue is knowing whether a Hellenization of Christian thought occurred, as Adolf Harnack thought, or rather as seems evident to me, a Christianization of Greek thought. St. John says literally "the Logos became flesh" (John 1:1). St. Paul was quite right to say that for philosophers any doctrine of this sort was "folly." When he wrote that Christ is Wisdom, he was not reducing Jesus of Nazareth to the philosophers' abstract concept of *sophia*. On the contrary, he was saying that the wisdom of the philosophers became Jesus, who made himself for us "Dei virtutem et Dei sapientiam" (I Corinthians 1:24). To allow the scientist's wisdom to annex incarnate Wisdom is not to redo a second Gospel revolution, but to dilute the first one. I do not speak of what Fr. Teilhard proposed to do, but about what he was doing against his deepest intention. But my words would have no meaning for him: to understand him as he understood himself, I am missing what is an irresistible feeling for him of the religious value of universal evolution. Christ the evolver is the only true Redeemer, because he *is* the redemption.

Irenaeus, the great adversary of the Gnostics: "The true gnosis is the teaching of the Twelve Apostles." I am not sure whether there exists an omega point in science. I do feel sure that in the Gospel, Jesus of Nazareth is completely different from the germ of Christ Omega.[17] Though Christ's new function has greatness and nobility, it is other than the old one. We feel ourselves a little as if before an empty tomb: they have taken our Lord, and we do not know where they have put him.

This attitude betrays the panic with which so many Christians are seized watching the de-Christianization of the modern world. They attribute it to the growing influence of science, and they would be right if it were proven that the proportion of the non-believing ignorant is lower than that of scientists who have kept the faith [translator: *sic*]. That is not at all certain. The masses whose loss to the Church is lamented did not neglect it for the temple of science. We would have to follow Teilhard if his doctrine gave the choice between faith without reason and indisputably demonstrated science, but the science that he proposes deals with objects generically different from those to which faith is devoted and, moreover, is not science. Teilhard gives notice to his readers to opt between the faith in the Gospel's historical Christ and a cosmic Christ in whom no scientist believes.

The solid and strictly scientific part of the work is not in debate. Science will assimilate it, and Christians will teach it as others do. The issue there is pure and simple paleontology and very few people are interested in it. The doctrine only begins to seduce the general public at the point where neglecting the austere paths of reason for the flowering meadows of the imagination, Fr. Teilhard passes from paleontology to fantasy. Worn out at this point, the scientists most sympathetic to his thought simply refuse to follow. Certainly, says the paleontologist Jean Piveteau speaking of the conclusions of a work that still stops well short of Christogenesis, "In this last part of his work, Fr. Teilhard de Chardin will seem to do the task of a philosopher rather than a man of science, and many who admire the paleontologist in his interpretation of the evolution of the living world will

17 All these expression of Teilhard de Chardin are found in Claude Cuénot, *Teilhard*, p. 142. St. Irenaeus's phrase is in *Contra Haereses*, IV, 33, 8, Migne, *Patrologia Graeca*, volume 7, columns 1077–1078. Other references are in Gilson, *History of Christian Philosophy in the Middle Ages*, p. 562, note 38.

have some trouble following the author in his anticipations.[18] One could not distance oneself from Teilhardian pseudo-science with more courteous firmness. At the precise moment when Teilhard wants to make us see how "the problem of God-Motor, Collector, and Consolidator ahead of Evolution is inserted"[19] into science, the scientist apologizes and takes leave of the Reverent Father. This attitude of the science will sufficiently warn us, if we did not know it by ourselves, that a different character has come on stage, and that the paleontologist has stopped talking.

We are told that this new character is the philosopher, but it is the philosopher's turn to apologize and take his leave. The philosopher's distrust is all the more on guard before the so-called philosophy because he sees clearly where it leads. We will only meet again with this Motor, Collector, and Consolidator of Evolution, keystone of the Noosphere in the Christosphere, beyond the theology of metaphysics and in the theology of religion. One would gladly position himself there, if the Christian theologian did not feel bound to make explicit reservations here. It is proposed to him "to integrate Christianity into Cosmogenesis,"[20] whereas for the theologian

---

18 Jean Piveteau, preface to Pierre Teilhard de Chardin, *Le groupe zoologique humain, structure et directions évolutives*, Paris: Albin Michel, 1956, p. XIV.

19 Teilhard, *Le groupe zoologique*, p. 162. The work concludes with the proposition: "If the pole of psychic convergence toward which Matter gravitates is arranging itself, itself out, were nothing else and nothing more than the totalized, impersonal, and reversible groping of all the cosmic nuggets of Thought momentarily reflected on others, then the World's winding up on itself would be deferred (by weariness of itself) in the same measure in which Evolution by progressing would take clearer consciousness of the impasse into which it flowed. Under penalty of being incapable of forming the keystone for the Noosphere, *Omega* can only be conceived as the *meeting point* between the Universe, arrived at the limit of centration and *another Center*, still deeper. The latter is self-subsistent Center and absolutely ultimate Principle of irreversible personalization: the only true Omega..." (p. 162).

20 Cuénot, *Teilhard*, p. 145. This is what the same author calls, "re-edit St. John's feat through the identification of Omega, this kind of new Logos, and of the resurrected Christ." Cuénot admits that Teilhard's thought can be called gnostic, if one wishes, but he adds, "It is St. John's, whose Prologue is read at the end of every mass" (p. 163). It is completely the opposite. Where does Fr. Teilhard de Chardin say that Evolution became flesh and that it dwelled among

the issue is to integrate cosmogenesis into Christianity, but for Teilhard doing so would be to get bogged down in an obsolete theology, still conceived in the format of the old model *anima naturaliter Christiana*, instead of constructing that theology that the new model *anima naturaliter Christiana* awaits today.

* * *

So, without having wanted to, we have turned to the meta-Christianity whose explanation we sought in the doctrine. It seems possible to me to find it there; it even seems that we have effectively found it. The shock that the expression caused me still seems excusable, all the more because nothing prepared me to undergo the shock. I had not gotten over finding myself in the presence of a religious belonging to the Society of Jesus in search of something beyond Jesus Christ. But I was mistaken about the meaning of his words. He was not thinking of a new historical Son of God destined to usher in the era of a new dispensation. Christ of the Gospel, so dear to his piety and whom nothing else could replace for him, remains where he is. Bethlehem is always at Bethlehem, and Calvary stays at Calvary, but this Christ of history, precisely because he is historical, continues to live, and just as we have adored him under the form of the Word, which he received from St. John, we ought to continue to adore him, always the same, under the form of Christ the Evolver that science has just conferred on him. The meta-Christianity about which Fr. Teilhard de Chardin of the Society of Jesus was talking to me that day was therefore not an attempt at another Jesus who was hoped for beyond ours. There would be no new Incarnation but renewal of a now inadequate way of thinking about Christ and along with him Christianity.

Thus understood the proposition ceases to be unbelievable. Moreover, it is not that of a Reformer who invites others to subscribe to *his* doctrine,

us in the historical person of Jesus of Nazareth or something completely different? He does not tell the scientists: This Evolution about which you speak so much is in reality Jesus of Nazareth. But rather, This Jesus of Nazareth, of whom we have spoken so much before the advent of the neo-Logos, is really Evolution. For those of us who are not St. John and do not live in a kind of scientific enlightenment, it is necessary to choose.

because Teilhard hardly has a doctrine, but rather a way of feeling, and he cannot be said to have done anything at all to spread it. It is even wonderful that in our century someone should have believed he could galvanize the masses around the concept of evolution that, as beautiful and moving as it may be, does not address the same human feelings as the religious beliefs that he needs vitally. Scientific enlightenment and the cult of evolution a little bit in the manner of Julian Huxley's confused evolutionism, would invite him to conceptualize in imprecise language, though one of scientific appearance, a religious experience whose Christian depth and authenticity are beyond doubt.

This is why I see no danger in delay. Teilhardism is inseparable from Teilhard de Chardin's scientific and religious life. Linked to his person in the very way that Teilhard apart, there will never be a second example of Teilhardism. No one can be held responsible for what the press makes him say. For the readers of *Les magiciens du matin*[21] Teilhardism is one more curiosity among other dreams that feed their imaginations. As for more rigorous minds, but often ones who are badly educated in their own tradition, who find in Teilhardism at least provisional refuge to shelter their faith, why hound them out of it? Better to hold onto Jesus Christ for bad reasons than to lose him. As Claudel magnificently put it, when one cannot go to God standing, one goes on one's knees, and when one cannot go to God on one's knees, one crawls on one's belly. Too much para-science for too little true Christian wisdom; there, it seems to me, is the cause of the infirmity that Teilhardism suffers.

But who is at fault? The more I grow old in the familiarity with Christian tradition, the more I am struck by two things: the incredible ignorance in which we stand in its regard and the thoughtlessness with which we all believe ourselves entitled to dogmatize about subjects in which there is a right to do so only after being sure about the teachings of the masters who have gone before us. It is true that doctrine lives. The Church's Tradition is not only conservative; it can also be Creative Tradition. It is for the church

---

21 [Translator: This seems to be a slip of the pen or of the pun for Louis Pauwels and Jacques Bergier, *Le matin des magiciens*, Paris: Gallimard, 1960. This volume is a sort of manifesto of what its authors called magical realism. Pauwels and Bergier, incidentally, later founded the magazine *Planète*.]

to be watchful here, and each Christian can suggest the possibility of new expressions to designate new developments. What does a Council do but that, after all? But precisely the spectacle that a Council offers, where the whole hierarchy is at work under the Pope's authority, makes us see how difficult the task is even when carried out in the most rigorous conditions of fidelity to tradition. Because it is certainly the latter that is at work and that continues.

This is not the way of the crowd of minor, private philosophers, Christians or not, who lightheartedly accept the heavy responsibility of introducing young minds to philosophical discipline. There are no longer mathematical formulas to transmit, physical laws to define, biological chemistry to teach. Each expression is burdened with a mystery by which the mind must be measured. Being is not a genus. There is something easy to say, but how to understand and make understood that this transcendental descends into genera and into individuals? Every error about the concept of being, or rather any negligence in the effort to discern its outlines, embarks the thought of professor and students upon false paths from which they will never return. Badly equipped, misled by the false assurance of missing philosophical competence, too many inventive but unproductive minds hurl themselves in good faith into speculative adventures that end as mishaps. We live under the regime of, "personally, I think that." One cannot help saying to himself, I certainly see what he *thinks*, but what does he *know*?

The most curious thing is what our professors refuse to do for the philosophy is what they admire in the teaching of science. It is necessary to learn philosophy as physics is learned, in order to be able to invent in one's turn. It is necessary to immerse oneself fully in a tradition to make it live and grow, modestly, by some new light. The medieval masters, those Scholastics scored today, could not know what was not known in their time, but Kant still admired their method. They did not permit themselves to use terms without defining them. Their students would not have permitted them to do it. Where is that fortitude of thought today? What a let-down when one descends from the terse rigor of the old masters into the gelatinous prose of our contemporaries.

Surely the remedy exists, but perhaps it is not within our power to apply it. If it only depended on us to have another Albert the Great, we would no doubt get him, and that would considerably increase our chances of once again finding pupils of a lineage related to that of Thomas Aquinas. We can only pray that God may give them to us, but the personal responsibility of each of us is also in play. Therefore, let each professor measure his own responsibility and watch over his own teaching, because if we continue to suffocate those pupils in embryo, perhaps God will be discouraged from granting them to us.

V

The Difficult Dialogue

The word dialogue is in vogue. I regret to say—not having myself any of the virtues of a skilled dialoguer, which are not to listen to what is being said and to take it in a sense that makes it easy to refute. It is a chimerical hope that there should be two people who proceed otherwise. So, I am not surprised that the only known good philosophical dialogues are of the Platonic kind, which are dialogues in one voice, where the same person puts the questions and answers them.

Nonetheless, I was touched to receive a little book, embellished with a personal dedication to which I am quite susceptible, because in it the author expressed his wishes "to have [my] opinion." Having no authority to speak in name of the Council or even speak about it, I will content myself with thanking Roger Garaudy,[1] while telling him briefly why the dialogue to which he invites me does not seem useful or even possible to me.

But I kept the book, not for its content, because it is as foreseeable as our Apostle's Creed, but because of how surprising the very fact of its publication is. If the Communist party were in power in France, such a book would be no more published than if the President of the French Republic were the Father Torquemada. To tell the truth, the undertaking seems meaningless to me. It must have a meaning, if not philosophical and religious, at least political, but only being able to conjecture, I have been silent until an article in *Figaro* (Wednesday, June 8, 1966) signed by David Rousset, seemed

---

1 · Roger Garaudy, *De l'anathème au dialogue. Un marxiste s'adresse au Concile*, Paris: Plon, 1965. [Translator: The numbers in parentheses in the text remit to the pages of the American version *From Anathema to Dialogue: A Marxist Challenge to the Christian Churches*, foreword by Leslie Dewart, translated by Luke O'Neill, New York: Herder and Herder, 1966.]

to me to open a window and give this tiny incident intelligible meaning alien to its own perspective. Let me first quote in its entirety the opening of this article titled "Moscow Prepares Substitutions in Europe."

> The East German Communists are taking the initiative in an approximation to the Social Democrats, and persist despite extreme difficulties, numerous obstacles, and unquestionable resistance in their own ranks. The French Communists stubbornly work to integrate their party into a kind of confederation of leftist movements and despite every rebuff, do not rest until the closest relations are established with the French Section of the Workers International, and to get there, even though embarrassed by the rigidity of their leadership, make or hasten to make concessions that are not just verbal but practical. The great majority of Italian Communists really seek the establishment of a single party including all socialist and Christian or other reformist tendencies, into which their own organization would be dissolved. In this way, in all the crucial sectors of Western Europe, Communist parties undertake a broad drive for unity. Such a phenomenon, and one so widespread, supposes a deliberate, coordinated common strategy. I maintain that a very important watershed in Soviet policy in Europe is being revealed.

I have no competence or opinion on the political facts reported in this passage. Their interpretation totally escapes me. Speaking simply as a reader commenting on the newspaper, I would simply say that the panorama painted by David Rousset seems to fit the publicly known facts well. Still, as a reader of Roger Garaudy, I do think I have the right to say that if David Rousset's hypothesis is well grounded, it situates this address of a Marxist to the Council in its place and its order within the overall policy that Rousset described. Moreover, this address connects with the extended hands, meetings, and forums where so many lay Catholics, priests, and religious want to let themselves be indoctrinated in the simplicity of their hearts. They believe they perform an apostolic work, but St. Paul did not go to the Areopagus to dialogue with the Greeks. He went to spread Christianity to them. Having said only what he knew better than anyone, he emerged from that encounter as solid as he was when he entered it. The Acts of the Apostles does not say that he converted the Areopagus, but at least he was not converted either.

According to reports that have come back, some of those who have taken part in dialogues do not seem well educated either in their own Christian truth or in the official truth of Marxism-Leninism. So, impelled by the facts that David Rousset described, I have come to be convinced that it might be useful to discuss clearly what Garaudy's address to the Council leaves in the shadows. Let us recall that the issue is simply to know what sense the dialogue to which we are invited has, if it has one

1. That Which is Essential

Without encouraging preconceived suspicions, it might be asked what the intention of this rather unexpected offensive is. Its ultimate reasons elude us, but a Communist never speaks at this level without committing the Party. It can be said, at least, that everything is taking place as if this doctrinal initiative fits into an overall plan with a view to common political and social action.

Garaudy locates the discussion at the level where politics is rooted in ideas: "Because in such a debate it is not possible to put one's conception of man into parenthesis in order to debate politics exclusively. Marxism, like Christianity, does not separate social and political problems from philosophical problems." Responding, it seems, to Jacques Maritain's memorable address to the UNESCO, Garaudy does not even think that we could be content here with an understanding at the level of practical reason and of the immediate requirements of what is good. Such empirical agreements, at present, remain burdened with too many speculative reservations that make as many heavy threats weigh upon the future. We are certainly dealing here with preparing a long-term future common action. Our Marxist is impeccable in his own orthodoxy because his thought moves completely in the order of *praxis*, and the point is certainly to change the world, to know it, of course, but in order to change it. Accordingly, the appeal for speculative dialogue is intended to create conditions favorable to the most extensive collaboration possible. "When we face the problem of combining forces for the building of the future together, cooperation in mutual trust is going to be possible only if the measures taken and the institutions created, the *means* adopted take on meaning and value in terms of conscious *ends* which, even though not identical, are at least acceptable to both parties" (37).

For my part, I see nothing objectionable in these demands, because they are exactly the same as what Christians ought to enquire before committing themselves to any cooperation whatever with an undertaking of Marxist inspiration. Like Roger Garaudy, I must "refuse to put [my] conception of man between parentheses and to limit debate to politics" (19). Likewise, I am in agreement that, concerning the human condition, "a dialogue so conceived is a demanding dialogue" (37). Let us understand by that a dialogue that, provisionally setting aside secondary practical difficulties, goes directly to the heart of the problem. "A dialogue of this kind demands of each of the participants a fundamental return: for the Christian as for the Marxist, there must be a passing beyond the historical and transitory so as to pinpoint what is essential and susceptible of no compromise whatever" (38). Only, when we remember that what cannot be the object of any compromise here is the concept of man, we wonder whether any agreement is possible on this question that cannot be the object of any compromise.

Perhaps a slight reproach of Roger Garaudy could be allowed at this point. He is too good a rhetorician. After having so clearly posed the fundamental condition at the start of his book, he enters the thickets of history, economics, and especially exegesis of Marxism, as if these were not some of those secondary questions about which, since Marxists themselves are not always in agreement, it is neither necessary nor fair to want our assent. There is a Marxist scholasticism as convoluted as the other one, in which we may be excused from participating, since it does not concern us. I also find amusing that Garaudy should want to convince us by citing Dominicans and Jesuits in his favor, when they are not Popes. There, he enters into a world in which we find ourselves at least as well as he does, but for my part I cannot erect one Marxism against others, be it Karl Marx's own, really or supposedly. If a Marxist invites me to dialogue, I can only deal with his own Marxism, and if the notion of man is its center, with his own notion of man. It turns out that the answer to that question posed on page 19 is found, after chapters of suspense, on pages 95–96, and this time in terms as exact as could be reasonably hoped for. But to understand the meaning of the answer, it is necessary to go back to the memorable Salzburg Congress.

Replying to one of our author's questions, Fr. Jules Girardi declared: "M. Garaudy asks us whether Christians think that Marxism impoverishes man. We answer him frankly: In the measure that Marxism believes that the earth can be enough for him, yes, it impoverishes him" (93). As could have been anticipated, Garaudy rises up against this vigorously, but in terms that make us see the dialogue's futility clearly, because he first answers that, "Marxists are so little content with the earth that they assume the primary task of transforming it" (93), and not only what is material but also in the order of the spirit. Marxism also proposes to accomplish "a profound spiritual metamorphosis of man" (93). There, as a result, our dialectician is safe, because he responds to an objection that has not been made. He is asked whether he does not think that in the measure in which Marxism believes that the earth is sufficient for man, it does not impoverish him. He answers that the Marxist man is not happy with the earth as it is. But this is not the question. The issue is to know whether, once the Marxist paradise is installed on earth and continuing on the path of indefinite progress, man will be as rich as the poorest and most unfortunate men in whose heart there still lives an unquenchable confidence in the Christian God.

Accordingly, for the Christian the real question is to know whether human nature is such that man can suffice unto himself. And since our Marxist refuses any "evasion" here, he will pardon us for leading him back to the question that was posed. Not, whether men are happy about the earth as they find it, but rather, does Marxism impoverish man or not? In other words, is the Marxist man poorer than the Christian man or not? In still other words, is the man without God, and accordingly without any other means, support, or goal than himself, as rich as the Christian person who finds his end and support in God?

The Marxist answer to this question is unambiguous. Yes, the man without God is still noble and rich. But this confidence in the sufficiency of human nature is affirmed in a very curious way: "We are undoubtedly living, Christians and Marxists alike, the exigency of the same infinite, but yours is presence, while ours is absence" (95). I confess that I do not understand. Is it enough to affix the minus sign instead of the plus sign to the infinity in order to achieve the transition from the condition of Christian man to that of Marxist man? But if the presence of the infinite can be changed into absence without impoverishing man, what then could impoverish him? Let us, furthermore, listen to our Marxist: "Is it to impoverish man to tell him that he lives as an incomplete being, that everything depends on him, that the whole of our history and its significance is played out within man's intelligence, heart, and will, and nowhere else, that we bear complete responsibility for this, that we must assume the risk every step of the way, since, for us atheists, nothing is promised and no one is waiting" (95).

Garaudy defends himself here from any suspicion of pride and rightly. I know this situation. I have lived it more than a hundred times that I disembark in a port or at a station, my baggage in hand, in a country where no one was waiting for me; I watched with a little tug at the heartstrings other travelers received by the joy of their relatives, their children, or the more discrete and more private joy of their wife. No pride assails us when nothing is promised us but the customs agent, and when no one waits for us but the completely impersonal reception desk at the hotel. I do not feel aggrandized or elevated by that loneliness, rather I am sad. Indeed often in those cases, before long, I go into some nearby church, because there I am certain: someone is waiting for me. I have only to sit down before him to feel myself less alone without it being necessary for me to speak to him.

I am not arguing, I narrate, and like Fr. Girardi at Salzburg, I only ask whether the man to whom nothing is promised and whom no one awaits is more or less rich than the one whom we Christians call "the holy man Job," and whose cry end by bursting out from the depth of his suffering, an incomprehensible cry for a Jew, almost absurd, but triumphal: "I know that my Defender lives" (Job 19:24). What glosses on these simple words! Our Marxist will doubtless add his own: "But if this Defender does not exist?" "I think," he says, "that Marxist atheism deprives man only of the illusion of a certainty, and that the Marxist dialectic, when lived in its fullness, is ultimately richer in the infinite and more demanding still than the Christian transcendence" (96). You *believe* that, dear philosopher, but what do you *know* about it? I do not know what standard you use to measure transcendence, nor how you can *know* that the dialectic that you live is richer than the transcendent that you do not live. I will not ask you whether to withdraw from man the illusion of a certitude is not to impoverish him when that is all that remains for man in order not to despair. I do not want to abuse your prudent "I believe," which may be only a reservation out of courtesy, but in the end the fact that you speak ceaselessly in the name of science as others do in name of the Bible. You do not know that Job's Defender is not living. You do not know—what is called knowing—that there is no God. In the presence of a spontaneous belief of man, so profoundly rooted that the Marxist state itself does not succeed in uprooting it, you know well that you have nothing to oppose, I do not say no argument, but no rationally necessary demonstration of the opposing thesis. So I came back to my own question: whether our dialogue ought to be or not be demanding. If the issue for the Christian as for the Marxist is to sort out what is essential and could not be the object of any compromise, have we not already reached the end of our dialogue? We Christians believe there is a God; we even think we know it. You Marxists believe there is no God, and no doubt you also think you know it, but you do not really know it, and even if you knew it, you would be incapable of imposing your certainty. Therefore, each of us stays with his own position and if our preliminary agreement was required for us to be able to work together to make the earth more fit for men, no hope of cooperation will be permitted. Such cooperation is possible, provided it is between man and man, not between Christians and Marxists. Perhaps we can economize here on superfluous dialectical elaboration. I only say to the Marxist, even on the level of simple practical reason and of earthly good, Christians cannot act in agreement for you, if for that it is necessary that they should subscribe to what is for you as for them the essential point, this Marxist idea of man, "which could not become the object of any compromise."

2. A Millennial Dispute

"The conflict between us," says Roger Garaudy, "is of a thousand years' duration." We shall not be able to dispose of it unless we face it frankly. A balance sheet of grievances was drawn up in Marx's lapidary phrase of 1843: 'Religion is the opium of the people' (96). After which with a serious objective tone that confers beforehand a completely impersonal value on what follows our philosopher continues: "It is well worth asking the question whether it is true from a purely historical and sociological point of view that religion is and has been an opium for the people" (97). Then the verdict comes regretfully but implacable: "It seems impossible not to answer in the affirmative" (97).

At this point Roger Garaudy enters into an essentially sociological and historical demonstration without appearing to realize that what he demonstrates is completely different from what he believes he proves. He understands he is demonstrating by the teaching of the Fathers, the theologians, and the Popes that if religion *is not just* the opium of the people, it is *also* that. But not for an instant does he ask himself what opium is, if its use is beneficent or harmful. In short, he starts from the assumption that to label something opium is to call it bad. I beg pardon for descending to this level and speaking with a philosopher by disputing a rhetorical figure, as if a comparison were a reason, in opposition to the scholastic adage. But after all, the fault is in Marx. Therefore, I will quite simply ask him whether he is not making opium responsible for the pain it soothes. And whether he does not blame the physician who, in the presence of a patient racked by the pain of nephritic colic does not advise him to take action, to become indignant, to rebel against his pain, but is satisfied with simply administering to him what a doctor friend of mine called "a beautiful and good injection of morphine." To which he used to gravely add, because he had literary education: *Ultima ratio medicorum!* In blaming religion as the opium of the people, Karl Marx makes religion responsible for evils that religion, knowing the evils to be inevitable and in any case present, simply helps people to bear.

The argument goes further than is thought, and it is extraordinary that some Christians let themselves be impressed by the reproaches made against one of the most wise, even most profound teachings of their religion.

Let us first note that when Marx reproaches religion for being the opium of the people, he ought at least to make an exception in favor of some religions. Islam is one of them, because Muhammad certainly did not put his people to sleep. But we would not settle a dispute by joining another one to it, and so I would simply say that for those of us who care about Christianity, the warlike misuse that so many *very Christian kings* have made of it is to be regretted rather than the so-called lethargy into which their religion would have plunged them. But that is not the question. Marx does not speak of peoples but of people, which in practice he identifies with the working class, that is, the class above the *Lupenproletariat*, and more generally speaking with all those exploited by the capitalist regime, whoever they may be.

The Church goes much farther back than the capitalist period. From slavery to serfdom and to the working class, she has always seen that there were exploiters and exploited. She has never forbidden nor even advised the exploited against seeking to make themselves free, but she has always advised against violence, because, as a general rule, it only makes their evils increase. This is not the place to discuss this question, for whose solution I doubt that there is a demonstration. One would not dare affirm that violence never produces beneficent results, but it seems reasonable to say that the good done with violence might have been done without violence or with less violence and that great suffering would have been avoided for those whose evils it was rightly desired to relieve. The French Revolution is an example. The hijacking of the Russian Revolution in benefit of the Bolshevik Party is another, because both were no doubt necessary, but it was not necessary that both should end in bloodbaths. Since such verbal reflections do not lead to anything definite, let us consider more closely two of the testimonies criticized by Roger Garaudy, as he himself reported them.

> The basic thesis will be developed in all its generality by Pope Pius X on December 18, 1903: "Human society, as established by God, is made up of unequal elements... Accordingly, it is in conformity with the order of human society as established by God that there be rulers and ruled, employers and employees, learned and ignorant people, nobles and plebeians."
>
> There evidently flows from this thesis a social doctrine based on resignation. The encyclical *Quadragesimo Anno* explicitly drew this conclusion: "The workers will accept without rancor the place which Divine Providence has assigned to them." (98)

May I confess that I see nothing scandalous in these propositions and that I even believe that at bottom Roger Garaudy is more in agreement with them than he says? For, in the last analysis, I imagine him living under a Marxist regime and calling together a Factory Council. Is he going to recommend to the workers only to accept with rancor the place the State has assigned them? But the issue is exactly that. Instead of "God," read "the society established by human beings who get their nature from God," and nothing changes. In Russia too, as I have seen it, society is composed of unequal components. The names have changed, but the social conditions have remained with every kind of inequality due to nature and there, as elsewhere, reinforced by the established political and social system. The Russia of the Soviets has its rulers and its ruled. It is better to be ruler than ruled. The majority goes on foot, and some go by car. Some dispose of more material resources than others, and that is by State institution. In principle, one is not born more noble there, but one becomes so. The learned are distinguished from the ignorant as elsewhere, and great artists, there as elsewhere, go through the world like lords, stuffed with bourgeois gold that no economic or social regime disdains. The hotels where I stayed were in ruins, and the trains on which I traveled were infested with vermin, but it was vermin in first class. I was not so stupid as to be astonished by that and do not have the hypocrisy to make Marxism responsible for conditions that, being simply human, are not of its making. I simply request that religion and the Church not be made responsible either. Finally, I beg that someone may please tell me, when humans are submitted to the Marxist form of these natural and social inequalities, what they should or can do to accommodate themselves to them.

Completely full of his ideal, Garaudy does not set himself a question that perhaps he thinks does not concern him. He would be happy under a regime thus in conformity to his desires and which, it may be hoped for him, would personally only bring him honor and profit. But, what about others? Many years ago, I asked the People's Commissar of a Russian university town the favor of meeting my colleagues from the local university. He agreed, organized the meeting and presided over it, something that my naiveté had not anticipated. Only then did I know what I had done, and I felt greatly embarrassed by it. We were all submitted to police surveillance, and clumsily, I had just made the fact come out into the open. After a few minutes of vain attempts to find a subject of conversation, I asked if I could help my colleagues in anything, especially with books that had small or non-existent circulation. A colleague expressed the desire to obtain Lavisse's *Histoire de France* for the University. I thought I could promise its shipment, but the commissar observed that we were dealing with a "bourgeois" history, and the project was immediately dropped. When I was alone and heading for my hotel that night, I heard a hurried step behind me. The person who wanted to catch up with me was one of my more discrete interlocutors. He stopped me under a light. He put his hands on my shoulders and said these simple words to me: "Let me look at you for an instant so that I may see a free man." My throat tightened. His hands dropped, and his hurried footsteps became fainter in the night.

I have never forgotten this brief encounter. I particularly think of it each time I ask myself what I could do if I found myself in a similar situation. At least I know well what the Church does not advise me to do. She does not advise me to revolt. She no more recommends revolution or recourse to violence than she did in other times to Christians under Nero. She would do exactly what Marxism reproaches her for doing. She would invite me to be resigned. No doubt I would remain free to pray, to hope, to do everything outside of violence to hasten the return of lost freedom, but because all power comes from God, she would not authorize any will to revolt in me. "There will always be," said Pius X, "princes and subjects." We do not always choose our prince. If he is a scourge, he is a scourge of God. He will meet his end like others before him. If Marxist regimes *could* tolerate religious freedom, true Christians would be their subjects. "To condemn the slave revolt in the name of love," is not "to make oneself accomplice to the master's oppression." It is to help the slave bear it.

3. Abuse of Confidence

It is sometimes difficult for me to think that cultivated and even philosophical minds really produce such palpable nonsense about the Church's teaching as the one that has just been denounced. It is a case where error in good faith becomes almost impossible to believe, Marxism not only blames religion for wanting to heal the wounds that Marxism itself inflicts, it presents itself as the source of all good, all progress in every order in the past, present, and future. It is granted that the Church may have rendered some service here and there, especially through its heretics or those judged to be heretics, but the great motors of progress are science and reason, whose spirit is the same as Marxism's.

We will not be able to enter into the swarm of arguments, all rhetorically skilful but each presenting some fact, true or not, swaddled in a tendentious interpretation. To the contrary, we must denounce clearly the endeavor to falsify history to which Marxism abandons itself to justify its theses.

The Church's civilizing role everywhere it could reach seems to me difficult to deny, but it is true that its primary task has never been to create and spread civilization. Under all its forms, science, philosophy, arts, economics, and politics (I only name some of them), civilization is a this-worldly, temporal goal, different from the Church's except in the measure in which the Church judges it appropriate to associate civilization to its goal, which is human salvation. This measure is subject to debate. Errors can be committed. Several certainly have been, but it is not necessary that they occur. It might be said rather that they can only occur in virtue of a fundamental misunderstanding about the nature of religion and its specific object. The Church has effectively fomented civilizations and cultures, moreover very different ones, as a kind of by- product. Because the Church wants to save man, nothing that concerns humans is alien to it, but Christ did not forbid his apostles to save illiterates. Likewise he did not charge them with teaching the nations mathematics or physics. He did not even charge them with organizing states according to the rules of justice. He sent them to preach his message and baptize men in the name of the Father and of the Son and of the Holy Spirit. It is only appropriate to judge the Church on the way it has fulfilled this task.

Completely the opposite holds for Marxism-Leninism, which, for purposes of pure political propaganda, devotes itself to making us believe that science inspired Marxism-Leninism's birth, as well as its development, and guarantees its final triumph. This misrepresentation,[2] very effective with crowds, is a myth; one wonders how it is possible to believe it even while working to spread it. The Christian is asked to "reject any theological intrusion in the scientific realm," (122) something legitimate in itself, except

2   [Translator: The French actually says "Image d'Épinal," referring to a genre of woodcuts produced during the 18th and 19th century in Épinal and many other towns. The Épinal images became proverbial for giving an idealized vision of things.]

that Marxism appears as a perpetual and general intrusion into this area, to the point of wanting to appropriate science to its own benefit. This is why it dares to present itself as a science. This is a personal illusion of such incredible naiveté that one is tempted to see it as a betrayal of confidence toward the "people" that Marxism-Leninism makes a profession of serving.

Strictly speaking, science has nothing to do with Marxism-Leninism. The vast movement of scientific research and discovery that emerged from Greece and began anew on an unforeseeable scale starting in the sixteenth century has absolutely nothing in common with Communism, not even with its birth. Marx came too late for that. The rise of the social sciences including political economy dates from the eighteenth century. Marx's personal doctrine fits into it as a particular phase, as transitory as the others. Marx's doctrine is not its origin, nor does it determine its course. Even in the order of *praxis*, which is really Marx's order, it cannot be said that the undeniable progress achieved by the working class is due to him. The average standard of living of workers is incomparably lower in Marxist Russia than in the eminently capitalist United States of America. Everyone knows to whom this progress is due: not to Communism, but to the union movement. Wherever it has remained faithful to its own ideal, it has regularly contributed to the elevation of the standard of living of the union members. At every level, Marxist doctrinal propaganda reveals itself to be a mystification,[3] where one is drawn to suggest that the authors themselves are the first victims. Christians who believe in their own dogmas at least have the merit of knowing that the object of their faith is incomprehensible. They

---

3 The term does not seem too strong. I do not want to move here into the frequent criticism of Marx's historical predictions. A physicist who had been mistaken in scientific predictions to this degree would be permanently disqualified. But the problem is not within our competence. I only suggest that the skeptics read *Imperialism, the Highest Stage of Capitalism*, by Lenin, who is still closer to us in time. This booklet was published in Zurich in the spring of 1916. Fifty years have slipped by, during which two capitalist countries, Great Britain and France, have proceeded to liquidate their respective empires, as if the highest stage of capitalism was not imperialism but its destruction and abdication. During this time, Russian Marxism has constituted a Republic of Soviets that greatly resembles an empire based on force, whose cost in blood and tears only history will tell later.

do not claim to speak in the name of science. It is disturbing to see how the adherents to a doctrine whose author so clearly affirmed his intent to pursue revolutionary politics in practice, are transformed into the heralds of speculation so alien to reality.

It is difficult to believe what one hears. They only speak about "believing." "Faith in God," they say, "causes in the Christian the assent which we live as creation" (111). Are we to think that nobody invented anything from the first century of the Christian era until the birth of Marx? Asked what they have discovered in philosophy, they answer: "*The development of the sciences and technology*, as far as the theory of knowledge is concerned, leads to the general substitution of dialectic for intuition and also to the reconstruction of the entire theory of knowledge on the basis of the notion of *model*" (79). But every dialectic supposes terms between which it moves, and what are they but intuitions? As for the completely new intrusion of the cybernetic concept of "model," starting from which, "the entire theory of knowledge can be thought of today" (80), who will be made to believe that Marxism has discovered the concept in our times? Gaston Bachelard could be cited in this respect, but I have never heard him or anyone else say he is a Marxist. At such a late date why do they go looking for godparents for a truth that has been sure of itself for more than a century?

Seeking an answer to this question, we gradually come to wonder whether the mystification does not go further than we thought. Not only are we not told what the Marxist theory of knowledge is, but also what is implied is not the real theory. There is a good explanation. Namely that in our time, the real reason is not confessable among philosophers. It can certainly be enunciated, but no one will believe it.

It is helpful to turn to recognized authorities. It is true that the authority of Joseph Stalin, about whom I am thinking, is disputed today, but so is his successor's authority, and for my part, I have always found Stalin's booklet, *Dialectical and Historical Materialism* very instructive.[4] It is a brief

---

4   Joseph Stalin, *Principes de léninisme*, lectures given at Sverdlov University at the beginning of April 1924. I have in front of me the French translation, new edition, Paris: Éditions sociales, 1945. Two other copies are dated 1946 and 1947. Joseph Stalin, *Le matérialisme dialectique et le matérialisme historique*, new edition, Paris: Éditions sociales, 1945.

exposition of the doctrine drawn from the works of Marx and Lenin and presented in their original simplicity without any of the long-winded developments aimed at hiding from the Christian reader the place to which he is being led.

First and above all there is materialism. Marx's Marxism is inverted Hegelianism: "To Hegel, the process of thinking, which, under the name of *the Idea*, he even transforms into an independent subject, is the demiurge (creator) of the real world, and the real world is only the external phenomenal form of *the Idea*. With me, on the contrary, the ideal is nothing else than the material world reflected by the human mind and translated into forms of thought."[5] In this doctrine, *real* and *material* are two words to name the same thing, although, by definition, the immaterial is nothing: "Matter, nature, being, is an objective reality existing outside and independent of our mind; that matter is primary, since it is the source of sensation, ideas, mind, and that mind is secondary, derivative, since it is a reflection of matter, a reflection of being."[6] In other words, "thought is a product of matter, which in its development has reached a high degree of perfection, namely of the brain, and the brain is the organ of thought."[7]

In the foreword, the editor notes, "The work was first translated in 1937, three centuries after the apparition of René Descartes' *Discours de la Méthode* in 1637. They are two moments in the same effort, two works of the same stature." So we have Stalin as equal to Descartes. One always wonders whether those who say these things believe them or want to make them believed. I am afraid they do not believe them, but I do not know at all.

[Translator: I will quote from Joseph Stalin, *Dialectical and Historical Materialism*, New York, International Publishers, 1940, 1977. Taylor and Francis published a recent edition in English of *Dialectical and Historical Materialism* in 1985. The Sverdlov University Lectures in English are *The Foundations of Leninism*; University Press of the Pacific republished them in 2001. I suspect Gilson would be amused by the fact that Stalin's works get almost no respect, but those who reject them are divided between some who abhor what was written by Stalin and others who are convinced that Stalin used a ghost writer so that his works are not really by him.]

5   [Translator: Karl Marx, Capital, volume I, p. XXX, New York: International Publishers, quoted by Stalin, *Dialectical and Historical Materialism*, pp. 5-6.]

6   [Translator: Stalin, *Dialectical and Historical Materialism*, pp. 15–16.]

7   [Translator: Stalin, *Dialectical and Historical Materialism*, p. 16.]

On the relation of thought to being, that is to say, matter, of which Engel's said that this was "the ultimate question of philosophy," we will have to satisfy ourselves with the little that is given us. How the organization of matter could suddenly blossom into the immaterial, into thought, by dint of becoming complicated, we will never be told, but that is not important, since we are looking for the most direct possible expression of this philosophy around which it is hoped we may rally at least for common action.

But how would that action be possible since in authentic Marxism, consistent with itself, social and political realities only reflect material and real conditions? Dear old Joseph Stalin has no hesitation in this central part of our dialogue with Communism. Let us rather listen to him:

> ... if nature, being, the material world, is primary, and mind, thought, is secondary, derivative; if the material world represents objective reality existing independently of the mind of men consciousness, while mind is a reflection of this objective reality, it follows that the material life of society, its being, is also primary, and its spiritual life is secondary, derivative, and that the material life of society is an objective reality existing independently of the will of men, while the spiritual life of society is a reflection of this objective, a reflection of being.[8]

It is doubtless unnecessary to underline the shifts in meaning that permit Stalin to reach the desired conclusion: matter exists independently of thought *therefore* thought is a reflection of matter. The material life of society is an objective reality, *therefore* the spiritual life of society is only a reflection of being (and being is matter). What we ask is simply that people not talk as if Marxism could make accommodations on this point today without betraying its essence. It cannot authorize them, because if historical materialism is not the reverse of the coin of philosophical materialism, as Stalin has just told us it is, the whole edifice of Marxism collapses. It is very far from doing that. "Whatever is the mode of production of a society, such in the main is the society itself, its ideas and theories, its political views and

8   [Translator: Stalin, *Dialectical and Historical Materialism*, p. 20.]

institutions. Or, to put it more crudely, whatever is man's manner of life, such is his manner of thought."[9]

What marvelous simplicity! It would be that if it were not simplistic. For in the end, Stalin assures us that history knows five fundamental types of relations of production: the primitive communes, slavery, the feudal regime, the capitalist regime, and the socialist regime. I have never been able to understand nor get an explanation why Aristotelianism, born in a climate of slavery, could survive in the thought of a Dominican friar living at the height of feudalism in a "material world" as different from a Greek city as a thirteenth-century Christian monastery could be, then could achieve new life in a flourishing capitalist regime through the thought of a German philosopher like Franz Brentano in the nineteenth century, and lastly again find defenders, perhaps old fashioned but very much alive, in the person of philosophers like Jacques Maritain, for whom, however, Marxist naturalism has no secret.

But perhaps the lack of seriousness is on our side, because we ask the Marxists to speak like philosophers, while they hasten toward action. Some-one stumbles on a phrase of Heraclitus and exclaims: behold, everything essential in the doctrine was already discovered. If that person were taken at his word, he would be reproached for having demonstrated the transcendence of the spiritual over the economic, against himself, unless he maintains that in Heraclitus's time being (matter) was already in the state in which the German Jew Karl Marx was to re-encounter it some twenty centuries later. For historicism, what contempt for history! But that is not the issue. The tragedy of working conditions was only too real in Marx's time. Even today, if salaried workers do not defend themselves with firmness and lucidity, they will find nobody to defend them. It is quite understandable that a doctrine that makes them the salt of the earth and counts on them to assure indefinite progress in the future, easily finds a hearing among them. Even as a propaganda argument, this is not serious.

But our Marxist intellectuals are not industrial laborers. Although they carefully nurture the myth of class unity among industrial laborers and

---

9   [Translator: Stalin, *Dialectical and Historical Materialism*, p. 29. At this point Gilson inserts a note.] The texts cited will be found in Joseph Stalin, *Le matérialisme historique*, pp. 7, 13–14, 16, 25.

other workers, very few of them exchange the pen for the pickaxe. The words "philosophy" and "thought" certainly mean something more precise than those vague signs that they freely manipulate in their writings, as if Socrates had not taught us long ago that we must not talk before having defined the words we use. But perhaps the misunderstanding lies there. For the Christian the word *being* does not signify matter. Rather it signifies God, and that is why, returning once more to the last of Marx's theses on Feuerbach, the Christian wonders whether there is not a fundamental misunderstanding about the data of the problem. "Philosophers have only *interpreted* the world in various ways; the point is to *change* it."[10] Yes, without doubt Jesus Christ came to transform the world, but not socially, economically or politically, as Marx proposed to do. How many divisions does the Pope have, the Marxist asks. None, but he does not need them. He would not even know what to do with them. It is all too natural that materialism does not understand what is being talked about because according to materialism what is being talked about does not exist.

4. False Witnesses

Have we responded to the question that was posed? Assuredly not, and we had nothing to respond to it. The plans for a Marxist society have not been communicated to us. What their spokespersons really think can only be known to us in so far as they say it. We have no way of knowing in what measure they do say it.

Nevertheless, if we ask about their real intentions, it is for two reasons.

On the one hand, the Marxist initiative is so surprising and so bereft of meaning, that one cannot easily be persuaded that it is serious. But if it is not philosophically serious, it might become intelligible on the level of action, especially political action, which we have just been reminded is the specific goal of Marxism. In the event that the grand maneuver described by David Rousset is a reality, it is important that Christians do exhaust themselves in vain efforts to discern a speculative meaning to words that

---

10 [Translator: This is Marx's thesis 11 on Feuerbach. See, for example, *Karl Marx, Selected Writings*, edited by Lawrence H. Simon, Indianapolis: Hackett, 1994, p. 101.]

perhaps lack it. My personal failure to find that meaning proves nothing, but if others experience the same failure, it will become plausible that, faithful to its essence, Marxism is not precisely occupied in philosophizing but in maneuvering.

On the other hand, the mental confusion in which the maneuver unfolds involves its own dangers. There is no lack of young Christians, laymen or priests, who are as sensitive as Marxists to the suffering of so many of the disinherited, and are uneasy to see the Church keeping itself away from political, economic, and, still more, revolutionary action in order to devote itself completely to pursuing its spiritual goal. We understand them, but even the King of the Jews proclaimed that his kingdom was not of this world. Innumerable saints, religious orders, priests, and laymen, known or unknown, consecrated their lives to relieve deprivations, the worst of which, alas, have no remedy. When a great political party invites them to join in a common effort to attack the evil at its very root, they will be all the more strongly tempted to consent in the measure in which they can be made to believe that at bottom Christ's teaching and Marx's share the same concern for infinity.

There, it seems to me, is where a grave danger threatens generous souls who put their destiny at risk by imprudently promising others a human happiness that perhaps it is not possible to give nor, furthermore, to receive. They should not listen to the Sirens' song because the Sirens lure you onto reefs. Listening to these voices inspired by Moscow, it can hardly be doubted any longer that even in the ideological and political field they prepare "the European substitution." They summon us by showing us certain of our own people, who, if we follow, will set us on the road of Marxism. In that, Garaudy not only does his work, and he does it well, but he renders us a great service, because I do not doubt that his quotations are correct (the same university gave both of us good habits), and if they are, they forbid the Christian to shy away from a judgment to which he is compelled. It is conceivable that in order to encourage us to swell the ranks of the Party, a Marxist aware of their meaning should quote the words of a priest for whom, "The synthesis of the [Christian] God of the Above and the [Marxist][11] God of the Ahead: this is the only God whom we shall in the future

---

11   [Translator: two words in parenthesis appear in the American edition.]

be able to adore in spirit and in truth" (54). It certainly must be said to those who grasp the real meaning of such words that they would be an imposture if they were not meaningless, since there is no Marxist God. On the contrary, the denial of God is of the very essence of Marxism. If we were not really dealing here in the last analysis with a political operation, it would be astonishing to see the synthesis of atheism and the Christian God proposed with apparent seriousness.

First of all, those among us who identify with "Christian Humanism" are counted as giving testimony for Marxism. The equivocation is so crass that it will not be necessary to insist. If Christian humanism consists in exalting the greatness of man made in the image of God, destined to a specifically divine ultimate goal, and provided with the means necessary to attain it, there exist such humanism. It is what Jacques Maritain has rightly named "integral humanism." Marxist humanism is quite the opposite, being an exaltation of man without God and against God. The two doctrines have only an equivocal name in common. One is the negation of the other. Those who would like to make sure of it should read the Fr. Henri de Lubac's fine book, serious and tragic, on *The Drama of Atheist Humanism*. Such a lucid demonstration dispenses us from insisting on the subject.

We would like to be able to put the same trust in another witness cited by Roger Garaudy, Fr. Teilhard de Chardin. This is not easy, because we know that Fr. de Lubac's deep friendship makes him write book after book to persuade us that the famous evolutionist had a great heart, was a holy priest, a missionary, in short to convince us of all sorts of things we do not doubt. The only trouble the friendship causes us is that it forces us to clarify our position against a person about whom it would be preferable to say nothing, if we could. But, since they insist to the point of underlining his agreement with certain aspects of Thomistic doctrine, it certainly is necessary to observe that there is something suspicious in the reception that publications like *Planète* and Marxist thinkers like Roger Garaudy give to Teilhard's thought. Moreover, it is remarkable that the diversity of his defenders guarantees that there is not much in common between their thought and his. Their philosophical location is the atmosphere of all the massive undemonstrated and indemonstrable affirmations. It is the place where everything is in agreement, because, as they say, "everything that rises converges," an observation that is not verified where I come from by any stream of water and very few trees. But then I lack the sense of the infinite.

Fr. Teilhard de Chardin's orthodoxy does not concern me. I am not his judge, nor am I qualified to be, but when I see Marxist preaching nourished by Teilhardian cosmogony, or in Roger Garaudy's case utilizing Teilhard's teaching in confirmation of his own, I cannot remain indifferent. By dint of hearing it repeated that Marxism is a science, that this science is based on evolution, that evolution is the great truth of which Teilhard de Chardin became the apostle, and lastly that there is a great area of agreement between the Jesuit scientist's theology and Marxism, many readers risk letting themselves be persuaded, although they are perhaps not informed precisely about what science and theology, or Christianity, evolutionism, and Marxism are. Teilhardism is not dangerous itself. It helps certain souls, and that is all for the good, but it seems to me sufficient to let alone and dangerous to recommend it. Personally, I would not guarantee it as an authentic expression of Christian thought, so suspicious for me is the deep agreement between Fr. Teilhard de Chardin's Christianity and Roger Garaudy's Marxism.

Passing over the synthesis of God and not-God that our two authors recommend, not however, without observing that the Marxist knows his trade better than the Jesuit, we will still have to observe that everywhere that the defender of Christian evolution agrees with the tendencies of scientistic positivism, the Marxist is all too happy to give him his approval. Each time that this occurs, a Jesuit adorned with the halo of scientist agrees with a Marxist philosopher, to give us the impression that we ourselves are religiously as well as scientifically backward. It is not pleasant to be the object of this slightly disdainful self-importance. After having listened to Julian Huxley's scientifico-philosophical meandering in Teilhard's company, a Protestant theologian tersely expressed my own impression in a single sentence: "You are very arrogant, Mr. Huxley." Fr. Teilhard de Chardin himself did not reproach Huxley at all. He had been hanging from his lips. When I read what he thinks of my kind of Catholics, I sometimes feel the desire to ask him: "Aren't you just a little bit contemptuous toward simple Christians like us?" But this would be unimportant. The worst is that in wanting to liberate us from our anti-scientific prejudice in theology, Fr. Teilhard makes it fairly clear that he doesn't understand the question at all.

Roger Garaudy congratulates Teilhard for wanting to eliminate from theology everything connected to an archaic worldview (49). But no theologian can picture the world other than as the science of his time paints it for him. In relation to religious faith, that scientific version is contingent. The (rather confused) conception of the world that the twentieth century has fashioned will be archaic tomorrow. Theology implies no scientific conception of the world. In the always-imperfect measure in which the world of science is the real world, it is God who created it.

Roger Garaudy praises Fr. Teilhard de Chardin for having wanted to free conscience from certain dogmas: "When we try to live and think Christianity with the whole of our modern souls, the first resistance encountered always arises from original sin" (49). Do you perceive this touch of arrogance? If I am not in agreement, it is because I do not live or do not think my Christianity, or if I live it, I do not do so with my whole modern soul (like Fr. Teilhard de Chardin's), otherwise I would meet resistance, and it will *always* be linked to original sin.

I do not dare to give an answer, since I feel disqualified in advance: "If the dogma of original sin binds and weakens us, the simple reason is that it represents, in its present form, a survival of static views which have been outdated in our now-evolutionist way of thinking" (50). All this leaves me perplexed. I ought to be more modern than Fr. Teilhard de Chardin because, at least for the moment, I am still alive and still the dogma of original sin neither binds nor weakens me, since the only difficulty I find in it is categorizing it as dogma. In my eyes, alas, it is glaringly evident. There is something in the world that doesn't work. What has happened? In man, beginning with me, there is something muddled or twisted, because I am not what I would like to be, and it does not even suffice that I should want to be it for me to become it. Is this a dogma? It is a simple truth that is not even Christian. To be sure about this, I looked in the *Petit Dictionnaire Larousse* for the collection of usual Latin quotes, and I read this one that I was quite sure of finding there: *Video meliora proboque, deteriora sequor.* Ovid puts these words in the mouth of Medea (*Metamorphoses* VII, 20) touching upon the person whose intelligence shows him the way of duty and truth, but whom weakness and the lure of pleasure, nonetheless, sways toward evil. That is a Medea whom I understand, because I know what she is talking about. In fact, she talks like St. Paul, except that the latter goes further: "I cannot understand my own behavior. I fail to carry out the things

I want to do, and I find myself doing the very thing I hate" (Romans 7:15). It is not the dogma that muddles me, it is sin. The presence of the sort of rot that I find inside me like the worm in fruit is the very thing that only a primeval disaster can explain to me. If I am asked why I should be responsible for it, it seems to me that I know, because this original sin is the unbearable *fomes peccati* in me that young Luther first hoped to extinguish before adapting himself to it too well. What displeases Teilhard de Chardin is that "the idea of the Fall is, after all, basically nothing but an attempt to explain evil in a deterministic universe" (50). Let us grant that, but why "deterministic"? Creation, human fault through rebellion against God, breaking the first order, the history of the Chosen People for which the Savior will be born one day, birth, life, and death of Christ, coming of the Holy Spirit sanctifier and light of the new order—what is static in all that? Marxism makes the most of the "conservative implication of the conception of original sin and the attitudes of expiation and resignation that flow from it" (50). But what then has nourished that Europe, the living germ of the future world civilization, except the Church? Sometimes one wonders what Teilhard de Chardin knew of his history and of his religion.

The religious verbalism with which Fr. Teilhard was content is too obviously without relation to science, which is not concerned with these problems. But those who let themselves be snared will be victims of the old and sadly very effective tactic that consists in opposing to the rejected doctrine the same doctrine presented as the discovery of a reformer. Garaudy the revolutionary is delighted at this unexpected ally, who also dreams only of changing everything. How will we adapt the Church to the tasks that await it in the new world? "We can answer in one word:" Teilhard de Chardin declares, "by becoming for God, the pillars of evolution" (51). What does this mean? It means this: "In the past, adoration was to prefer God to things by referring them to him, and by sacrificing them to him. Adoration has now become our devotion body and soul to the creative act by associating ourselves with it for the fulfillment of the world through our effort and research" (51).

Even approved by his Communist commentator (with reservations), our theologian really says nothing new, or does not dare to say all he thinks. But all the same, he does not think that if formerly adoration was to prefer God to things, today it ought to be to prefer things to God. If the issue is always to prefer God to things, nothing has changed. I see Fr. Teilhard becoming impatient. "But yes! It is a question of attitude. Instead of remaining passive as formerly, we associate ourselves to the creative act through work and research." We think we are dreaming. Where did Teilhard de Chardin learn his theology? This passive notion of creation and of man that he combats is totally his invention. Was he never made to read *Summa Contra Gentiles*, book III, question 21? I fear not. Or has he read without understanding the texts of Dionysius and St. Paul cited by the Common Doctor there: *omnium divinius est Dei cooperatorem fieri* and *Dei adjutores sumus*? That is possible. In either hypothesis the result is the same. Our theologian sets his predecessors' own doctrine against them. Roger Garaudy is not part of this business at all. A Jesuit tells him that the Christian universe is traditionally static and that man does not cooperate in the creation. Garaudy believes it and observes that enlightened Christians and Marxists at least agree against this "fixism." He cannot be blamed for having believed it. He needs nothing more since, with Teilhard de Chardin, he proposes to join to what the latter admirably calls his flock: "the common front of all those who believe that the universe is moving forward and that our task is to make it move forward" (31). However, one does not know whether to laugh or cry seeing Jesuits and Marxists united in this "common front" with St. Paul, Dionysius the Areopagite, and St. Thomas Aquinas.

Let us stop here before setting foot in this doctrinal swamp where we are certain to get bogged down if we venture. Teilhard de Chardin finds that too much importance is attached to miracles (105).[12] I admit that one

12 [Translator: The book version of this essay corrects a mistake that appeared in the journal version. In a letter of June 22, 1967 to the Italian philosopher Augusto Del Noce, Gilson expresses his mortification at having wrongly attributed to Teilhard a blunt rejection of miracles that Garaudy had correctly attributed to Max Planck (*Caro collega ed amico. Lettere di Étienne Gilson ad Augusto Del Noce*, edited and introduction by Massimo Borghesi, Siena: Cantagalli, 2008, p. 85 for the letter in Italian, 124 in French, 153 French facsimile. Teilhard's mode of expressing himself about miracles was more ambiguous than Planck's—as indeed Gilson complains. For a sympathetic presentation of Teilhard see Thomas M. King, S.J., *Teilhard's Mass: Approaches to "The Mass on the World,"* Mahwaw, New Jersey: Paulist press, 2005. In 1909 Teilhard wrote an essay on the miracles at Lourdes, "Les Miracles de Lourdes et les enquêtes canoniques."]

should be on guard against false miracles, but the Church attaches no importance to them, whereas it attaches extreme importance to the concept of miracle itself. By contrast, according to Teilhard: "the thought of the miraculous no longer acts effectively on our minds" to such a degree that many Christians remain believers "not *because of* but *despite* the wonders related in Scripture" (106). That may be, but Jesus did his miracles as testimony to his divinity, not to make belief more difficult for us. Following St. Paul, we believe in Christ "made son of God," "according to the Holy spirit," "by his resurrection from the dead." We do not believe in our resurrection in spite of this but because of it: "If the dead do not rise, neither has Christ risen, and if Christ has not risen, vain is your faith. ... For since by a man came death, by a man also comes resurrection of the dead " (I Corinthians, 15:16–17, 21). And let us not speak in this regard of an "unexpected softening of determinisms." To soften death, if the expression has meaning is different from restoring life. The Father raises his Son from the dead by the Spirit, and his resurrection is not only the announcement but also the effective principle of our own. "Christ's resurrection," the Jerusalem Bible says, "is the very foundation of faith." How could we believe *in spite of* the foundation of faith? And his is not a miracle of softening, but of power. It would be easier for me to deny the miracle with Garaudy than to believe in miracles that are not miraculous with Fr. Teilhard de Chardin.

Can we usefully dialogue with atheists? I doubt it if they are Communists, and I even dread this dialogue if it is between Marxists as well informed about their doctrine as Roger Garaudy and theologians as badly informed about theirs as Fr. Teilhard de Chardin. In cases of this kind, the Communists absorb the theologians with the greatest ease and feed on them with advantage. Only the ridiculousness of the adventure remains to us.

No doubt there is a remedy. Leo XIII prescribed it along time ago, but the pull of each period and the currently generalized absence of metaphysical and theological training oppose practically insurmountable obstacles to the diffusion of truth. They become completely insurmountable when a badly situated apostolic zeal becomes the accomplice of so many hostile forces and believes it can domesticate them by yielding to them. Then we see Marxist atheism provide itself with weapons from the Catholic theologian, and it becomes possible indeed for a conversion to occur but inversely.

VI

Wandering Among the Ruins

It was a fine March morning under a bright blue New England sky, brisk and almost cold but invigorating. The weather invited one to go out onto the broad expanse of the College green. At its center I saw the new chapel. It was a good opportunity to hear Mass, and I arrived just at the beginning. So much the better because it was a low Mass, and until the canon, there was nothing to draw my attention. At that moment I noticed movement, the men and women present, all students of the Catholic college where I was, got up from their places and positioned themselves around the altar. I hesitated for a moment, but having no idea of what I was supposed to do in what is a new rite to me. I finally stayed in my place. The spectacle was curious because one would say that all the lay people of both sexes were concelebrating. Sometimes they said things, I know not what, and sometimes they were silent. I followed the service as best I could, not without feeling a little stupid, alone in the pew in the nave where I sat out of habit. At one moment they seemed to incline toward their neighbors touching the end of each other's fingers and murmuring some phrase, probably *pax tecum*. I told myself with satisfaction that not being involved I did not have to wonder what to answer, but that failed to reckon with the last woman among the faithful, who noticed me from afar. Incapable of tolerating such an uncommunal attitude, she came down the altar steps, out of the sanctuary, headed toward me without appearing to raise her eyes, took the ends of my fingers in hers, and mumbled a rather long formula that I did not understand, but which in no case could reduce to a *pax tecum*. Not knowing what to say, I stupidly responded: "Thank you, miss." But nothing seemed to surprise her. After a short waive, her hands joined and her eyes lowered, she returned to the group of communal faithful from which I had incomprehensibly been separated.

The incident is insignificant, but it touched me deeply. For the first time since my childhood, I had attended a Mass in a Catholic church according to a peculiar liturgy during which I did not know how to behave.

The scene changes. In a French village, a foreign priest wanted to make the necessary arrangements to say Mass next morning. I telephoned the pastor whose cordial voice set me at ease immediately. "At what times does your friend want to say his Mass? —"At eight."—"No, that is the time I say mass. Unless he wants to concelebrate?" I translated for my friend, but this proposition, however honest, seemed to upset him deeply. It took me a little time to understand that since the pastor did not know a word of English, and my friend hardly knew more French, neither would understand the other's Mass, which perhaps does not make concelebrating impossible, but promises embarrassing moments. We agreed on eight-thirty. The first missal that my friend opened had the Mass in French with the old Latin text in small letters in the margin, illegible for my friend. The parish did not have any missal in English. Who would believe it? They went to get a huge Latin missal from yesteryear, after which the pastor hurried off to his Thursday catechism class, and the Mass took place according to tradition. I was able serve it myself only because I had to respond not in French or English, but in Latin.

For the first time since my long lost childhood, I had just seen two Catholic priests incapable of understanding each other so as to celebrate a Mass in the same language. Once the unity of the liturgical language is broken, the language of the rite fragments according to the multiplicity of vernaculars. Catholic priests from different countries can no longer say the same Mass. It seems that there is nothing left but to resign ourselves to it.

This is not the most serious thing. Back in the United States in the fall of 1966, I quickly got the impression that the atmosphere had changed. In the American church where not long ago priests still decided everything, everything seemed to have been put into doubt. The laity itself was not much involved in this. Faithful to the old adage: *pray, pay, obey*, they continued to pray with fervor, pay with exemplary generosity, and obey without arguing. There, as in France, the multitude of the faithful, tranquil and content with its lot, watched the imposition of liturgical reform and resigned itself. Altars changed place. Facing the congregation priests now proceeded with all sorts of mysterious rites, repeated signs of the cross in all directions that, lacking meaning for anyone but the celebrant, from a distance resembled pious magic tricks. Since it pleased their priests, who formerly turned toward God and now turned toward them, the faithful could only follow, wondering, however, why these changes occurred, who decided them, and what rules set their limits. If there was a revolution, it came from above, which dispensed it from needing to justify itself. Moreover, the worthy public did not know everything. A layman who had just served Mass, was surprised one day to see the priest put together the hosts that had not been consecrated and what remained of the consecrated hosts that had not been consumed. His comment about it received the answer that this was not important. His memory recalled a story one of the priests who brought him up told him in childhood. During a fire, seeing the tabernacle threatened by the flames, the pastor hurled himself in to save the holy forms at the risk of his life. Whatever we think of the necessity of the action, its meaning was evident. We are far from that time, and laymen are astonished to learn that the distinction between consecrated hosts and others has become unimportant. Laymen have not invented these changes. On the contrary, they are astonished by them and do not understand.

Ideas are more hidden than rites. We see what people do, not what they think, and no doubt the most troubling source of perplexity for laymen is those ideas present in the priest's mind that justify his conduct for him and that his faithful do not know.

I was brought up on the old idea of the priest, not only centuries old but millenary, since all the priests who educated me, proclaimed themselves to be priests *secundum ordinem Melchisedech*. Incidentally, I owe to this childhood attitude my indestructible feeling about the substantial unity (begging pardon for this term that escaped me) of Judaism and Christianity. I do not want to oblige Jews to become Christian, but I will never be stopped from publicly confessing that my God is the God of the Jews. Educated in the Petit Séminaire de Notre-Dame-des-Champs, which welcomed future laymen and future priests, I saw one of my brothers, hardly younger than I, choose the priesthood. Many of my companions did the same. We used to say of them that they "had the vocation," and although recognizing what the signs were that one did have the vocation was not very clear to us, it was difficult to be mistaken about certain signs that one did not have it. Thus, frequently thinking about a local girl with the hope that you could marry her some day was considered a clear counter-indication. We were left with no illusion about the life of the priest, a life of sacrifice in every sense of the term, because the clergy freely renounces the world with some of its most legitimate aspirations and consecrates himself to God. *Dominus pars hereditatis meae.* I am one of those who did not have the courage to pronounce that formidable phrase. I believe I did well, because I would not have had the strength to keep to it, but I always knew what heroism it implied and what incomparable nobility it conferred on those who said it. The priest has remained a sacred being for me. What he is as a man is his business. For me he is always a person who one day of his life declared that the Lord is his inheritance, because it is as such that he is a priest, and the Church is right to say that, whatever he does or says thereafter, being a priest no longer depends on him. As a simple layman, I often think of the great saint of laymen, Francis of Assisi who "revered all priests," and I believe that everyone brought up in the same religion as I was still think the same, although some of their priests do not ask for so much.

I know such remarks may be naive; others would say worse. But at the rate these things are going, soon no one will know any more that they existed. The simplicity of such a state of mind is somewhat surprising. The first year I taught in an American university, one of my colleagues confided to me that what surprised him in our priests was their mode of dress. "Why don't they dress like everyone else?" I answered without hesitation, as if it were evident: "But our priests are not people like everybody else!" As he cited his friend, a Lutheran pastor who did dress like everyone else, I retorted a little surprised myself at my own indiscretion: "If he is a Lutheran, he does not believe in the sacrament of Holy Orders, so he is indeed a person like everybody else, and would have no reason to dress in a peculiar way." Evidently we are beyond that, and my argument of yesteryear would no longer come to mind, but these are things without importance, except as signs of a general tendency to erase the distinction between cleric and layman, a minor symptom of a growing desire to desacralize religion.

I am not surprised or scandalized that a priest should want to get married and do so. The Superior General of an American congregation, driving me in his car from the United States to Canada, employed a good three hours to explain to me that he was going to get married. I wished him all possible happiness, not however without drawing his attention to the

100

reverse side of the coin of which conjugal happiness is the face. In every order, we always suffer in the measure of our love. Great joys and great pain come from the same sources. So I did not raise any objection and contented myself with expressing my skepticism about the motive he alleged in order to deny that he was ordained a priest. "At the age of twenty-four," he said to me, "I was ordained without knowing what I was doing." That is very possible, if by that he understood, as I believe, that he had not yet discovered the human good he was renouncing. Cases could be mentioned where that discovery was still later. "The strongest part of the Tangible," Teilhard de Chardin said, "is the Flesh. And for man, the Flesh is woman. Embarked from childhood on the discovery of matter, it was inevitable that I should find myself one day face to face with the Feminine. The strange thing is only that the encounter should have waited to happen until I was thirty." This late feminine vocation is no obstacle to the other, and priests would be very unfortunate if the charm of feminine company, with the benefits it brings, were forbidden to them. How many Philotheas there are in the history of spiritual direction! But marriage is something else. Living in a time when the ideal of the clergy was still in full force, Abelard acknowledges straightforwardly that it is impossible to be at the same time completely for God and completely what a married man should be for his wife and children. The debate of the cleric Abelard with the husband of Heloise, to say nothing of the unfortunate child born of the union, still serves as an example. Last fall's newspapers do not let us forget it.

The question of priests marrying is beyond our competence in every sense. For Catholics only one authority has the right to decide it, the Pope. I once reported in *France Catholique* a conversation in which good Pope John XXIII told us how sensitive he was to the hardship celibacy imposed on some young priests. It is a real martyrdom for them, he said. I do not know how many newspapers all over the world reported that phrase, and did so accurately, moreover. But to my knowledge none of them reported the continuation of the Pontiff's remarks about the impossibility he himself saw of freeing these young priests from the burden of chastity. Could we give up saying *unam, castam ecclesiam*, he wondered? He answered no. I did no more than take note of this. I recall the statement only to note my surprise and to judge it symptomatic that the press would not have quoted it in reporting the preceding remarks so approvingly, but since then the question of clerical celibacy has become a veritable obsession. It is understandable that it should interest priests very personally, and lay people would be ill advised to demand a sacrifice from them that they themselves do not want to take. One simply asks them not to justify their decision by an *ad hoc* theology, since its real motives are only too easy to understand. One asks furthermore to understand if we tell that that lawfully married priests, furnished with all the Church's authorizations and consequently religiously and theologically irreproachable, will no longer be priests in the sense in which those whom we know today still are, entirely and exclusively devoted to God's service. But what use is it to act as prophets? The present has enough to occupy us.

Since these are the topics that hold our attention, we will indicate them here, insofar as they are known to us, at the same time as the decisions.

Time, January 6. 1967, "*Married*: Robert G. Wesselman, 38, former Roman Catholic Monsignor and official of the Belleville, Illinois diocese, who left the priesthood last October 24, and Françoise Burton, 36, divorced, mother of two children, at Hardin, Illinois, November 18." Wesselman, who intends to work in an anti-poverty program, says that he gave up the priesthood because the church had not succeeded "in being sufficiently identified with those who suffer discrimination."

Toronto Globe and Mail, December 17, 1966. "*Priests want freedom. No more celibacy! Roman Catholics Say...* A survey conducted this week in the United States revealed that 62 percent of Roman Catholic priests want the freedom to marry ... An unofficial survey of the same type shows that similar results would be found in Toronto, if the survey could take place officially... More than 60,000 priests have abandoned their ministry in the world, many of them in order to get married."

Anthony Girandola, a priest who married in 1965, has established a center at St. Petersburg, Florida, to help married priests. "We are like people shipwrecked and adrift in a lifeboat, waiting to be accepted by the Church." No special reason is given why he left the Church, but the photo of Mrs. Girandola and the baby published in the *Globe and Mail* the same day suggests the simplest explanation.

For more than a year, a theology congress to study the post-Vatican II situation has been planned by the English speaking Canadian hierarchy. It will take place in August 1967 at Toronto, Ontario. The organizers have the delicate mission of choosing qualified speakers from all over the Christian world. One choice seemed obligatory for England, that of Rev. Charles Davis, the best-known Oxford Catholic theologian, who accepted the invitation graciously. Nevertheless, on December 26, 1966, Rev. Davis called a press conference to announce that he was simultaneously leaving the priesthood and the Church. The news was as discouraging, *The New York Times* commented, as if the Beatles were dissolving their group because they did not like the sound of drums and electric guitars. Rev. Davis reproached the Church for being "a vast impersonal, inhuman system without freedom," which had become incapable of loving. That was evidently not his case, because at the same time he announced his intention of marrying Florence Henderson, 36, of New York, who had also left the Church. When Rev. Davis affirms that his personal experience has destroyed the idea in his mind that the official Church represents Christ's presence in the world, we readily believe him, but the future Mrs. Davis no doubt made her contribution.

The number of surveys of American priests has become so great that one ends by losing track of them. For instance, 5,936 priests of the Boston diocese were surveyed, that is to say "exactly one third of all the priests of the diocese who are not pastors or monsignors."[1] Three thousand forty eight answers to the questionnaire were received, and it was concluded, "sixty two percent of American Catholic priests believe that diocesan clergy ought to be free to choose between celibacy and marriage. The majority of those who favor this freedom hold that the freedom to choose ought to remain after, as well as before ordination." (*National Catholic Reporter*, December 14, 1966, p. 1)

An item from the France Press Agency datelined New York, March 27, 1966, mentions an apparently different inquest, since it had involved ten thousand priests in twenty five American dioceses: "A fourth of the priests

---

1   [Translator: I have been unable to locate the National Catholic Reporter article cited. But if the survey really referred to priests of the Archdiocese of Boston, the figure is wrong by a factor of ten. The Archdiocesan website gives the 1966 total for diocesan priests as 1429, the highest number ever. Possibly this was a national survey run from in Boston, where the priest-sociologist Joseph Fichter, S.J, was based around this time.]

questioned had already answered and 97 percent of them had declared themselves in favor of the following measures: first, that marriage be optional for members of the diocesan clergy; second, that religious who are priests and desire to marry be transferred to the secular clergy; third, that priests who have married be readmitted to the Church."

The previous survey invoked 3,048 responses from 5936 questioned to conclude about the opinion of American priests in general. This one drew its conclusions from the responses of a quarter of the priests surveyed to the opinion of ten thousand, three quarters of whom had not responded. I do not know what specialists in opinion surveys think of these methods, but I hardly worry about it, because we are told that this inquest owes its newsworthiness to the marriage of the Catholic priest Fr. Edmund Kurth to a former nun. The blessing was pronounced on them last Saturday, March 25 at Pewaukee, Wisconsin, "by a Lutheran pastor who refused to reveal to the press the location where the ceremony took place." The pastor did well, because Luther himself married a nun, but precisely for Luther, Holy Orders was not a sacrament and vows had no value. Accordingly, the Lutheran position in this case is completely logical. That of married Catholic priests, in any case, would be just as logical if in receiving the sacrament of Holy Orders, they had not made a vow of chastity.

A layman is not at ease speaking of these problems, which he strongly feels do not concern him. Only the Church can decide about them, and only those who are priests or propose to become priests qualify to express themselves on this subject. But the future of the clergy directly affects the faithful; first of all in their number, which is declining everywhere; then in their social situation, because we need to know whether the needs of individuals or of families are to be met; finally and above all in spirit, because a priest who owes himself to a family in virtue of the obligations emanating from the sacrament of marriage will no longer ever be able to become everything for everyone in the image of his master and even no longer *should* be able to do so.

So what is there behind this flight from the priesthood and celibacy that the priesthood imposes? The desire to marry, natural and legitimate in itself, is only one of the forces at work. In some cases the inhuman fashion in which ecclesiastical discipline is carried out causes useless suffering and irremediable discouragement. Many priests go away without saying anything. They can do no more. Crises of recruitment in all countries, decisions to get out of the convent simply because one is bored there, the sensation of lack of adjustment of the conventual lifestyle to the aspiration of modern men or women, all that occurs without fanfare, and no one would know anything if newspapers and magazines on the prowl for every occurrence outside the rules, were not at pains to inform the public about them.

Moreover, it is frequent enough that religious sisters, who become prominent personalities in their respective cities precisely thanks to their condition as sisters, take advantage of the first favorable occasion to secure an open position in the secular world, which—essential point—allows them to serve the Church better than in the orders. They leave the orders to remain faithful to their vocation.

After sixteen years of religious life in the Sisters of Notre Dame of Loreto, Marilyn Morheuser left the order for a secular position in Milwaukee. The January 13, 1967 issue of *Time* from which I take this item, mentions that in the diocese of New York alone, forty-seven sisters left their convents in 1966, twice as many as in 1965. Moreover, we are not dealing with young women put off by the rigors of communal life, but with mature women who already have long experience of religious life behind them. Speaking of her life in the convent, Sister Morheuser says, "I was happy, but it was as if I were in a box with windows. You see things happening outside. You want to help, but cannot because you are enclosed in the box."

Accumulating occurrences like these proves nothing, but proving something is not the issue. The very spirit of these upheavals is what matters, because it is its own lesson. Jacqueline Grennan, 40, Notre Dame of Loreto sister, President of Webster College in Missouri, is the only woman on the President's Council on Education. She is a well-known, respected figure in the world of American Higher Education. But we were informed at the beginning of January 1967 that she was leaving her order after 18 years of profession. The idea came to her in 1965 when she was asked to lead the war on poverty. At that time Sister Grennan asked herself whether she felt free to head an anti-conceptive campaign, and her answer was that being under the vow of obedience, she had lost the right to make her decision herself. The most extraordinary thing is that Sister Grennan, in becoming a lay educator, proposed to laicize Webster College, and that, while waiting for a decision from the Vatican Congregation for Religious, the Loreto sisters decided to entrust the control of Webster College to a lay board. These things only happen in America, but they do happen there.[2] May I add that I often admire how they happen there? No useless tragedies. Everything is done so that the sisters who so desire can leave their convents without leaving the Church. Dispensed from their vows by Rome and not having the indelible character of the priesthood, they can marry or not, and some of them only come back more gladly to revisit their old convent when they are not obliged to stay there.

This apparently idyllic situation nonetheless masks much struggle, suffering, and in the last analysis a too real disorder in consciences. The most comprehensive idea that can be applied to the overall panorama of these events is that of secularism, understanding by that a generalized tendency to prefer the lay to the priestly everywhere and the temporal order to that of the Church. It is self-evident that this is often useful or even necessary. Every time a disciplinary problem is involved, we end up seeing that the necessary freedom for temporal activities is not easily compatible with the Church's moral and religious demands. That is so even though the Church sometimes invites its religious or its priest to take on responsibilities that the Church wants him to assume, without feeling herself entitled to entrust them to him. "Do it, provided that I don't know anything about it." Uncertainty likewise hovers around the best way of serving God, and often there is a preference for solutions that favor the temporal at the expense of the spiritual. The spiritual is betrayed in its own interest, when those involved do not come to convince themselves that the spiritual has the duty to commit suicide.

Nothing is as ugly as an *ism*. So one does not dare to look for an *ism* to label the vast current that carries contemporary societies, minds, and hearts further from the Church each day. We are not dealing with paganism, because the historical pagan state was cluttered with gods, rites, and priests. Today the worthy Polyeuctes would find no more statues to smash except for that of Marianne in the town halls of the French republic, which only presides over future births. The French State is secular by virtue of the constitution itself. The Chief of State can believe what he wants. The state itself

2   I take the information from *Time*, January 27, 1967, and January 13, 1967. The articles are titled "Another Nun Defects" and "The Restive Nuns."

is secular. So, by consequence of a history in which the French citizen has not taken part and against which he can do nothing, each French citizen is condemned to live his whole life as a Frenchman in complete divorce from his religion. The country for which he is ready to die, if necessary, no longer wants to hear anything about the religion that helped so many Frenchmen to give their lives for it. In France, the highest temporal good officially takes no notice of the highest spiritual good of millions of its citizens. This collective schizophrenia, typical of every disintegrated society, is so contrary to nature itself that vast political parties flooding over national boundaries nowadays unite multitudes that thirst for any universal and absolute good that takes the place of a religion without being one. That, moreover, is why Communism so effectively reinvents a Church with its believers, its dogmas, its doctrinal intolerance, its virtues and its vices. The Communist multitude chants its own *credo* and permits no one to improve its expression. When a Marxist Council has spoken, everyone knows what he must think and do. The fate that awaits him if he rebels very much resembles what the Holy Inquisition reserved for heretics. A sign of adhesion lets Marxists recognize each other. It is not a cross that promises salvation but a clenched fist that threatens. Caught between an officially atheist State, a political mass movement whose triumph demands the destruction of religion, and that personal faith in God that refuses to die in him, the French Catholic is a person broken by his environment, a citizen without a church, a Christian without a fatherland. The priests who celebrate high Mass do not officially remember either France or its leader in the *memento* of the living. This inner fissure goes down to unsuspected depths within the majority of Frenchmen themselves. The government campaign against Christian schools is only its visible sign, because in a country where free-masonry established its empire, there are places where, even if he longs in is heart to do so, no public school teacher dares to set foot in church. Conversely, a person holding a doctorate from one of many universities and member of many foreign academies could live in a small French town for thirty years without once being invited to cross the threshold of the public school. His presence would soil its secular purity. *He goes to Mass*, he is pestiferous.

Education in Christian schools, where it remains, can only suffer the effects of this situation. We can dream about a country or state that suddenly became intelligent and supported all confessional schools of whatever affiliation they might be in order to mobilize all religious forces to its advantage. Then, it would become legitimate and healthy that the secular school itself should be a confessional school, the seminary as it were of militant rationalism. We never know how things will turn out. The little pupil of the "lay school" might be named Charles Péguy. Jesuit secondary schools prepared many contributors to Diderot's *Encyclopedia* and fomented Voltaire's strange anti-religious religion. What is essential for a country to live is that it believes in something beside itself, and whatever its political form may be, it will never have only believers to serve it well. The choice is not between those who believe in God and those who do not believe, but rather between belief in God and faith in atheism. Marxists know it, and St. Augustine endeavored to persuade the pagan empire of his time of it. A country is only well served when there is something above it.

Such concepts are chimerical in an age when the temporal is everywhere affirmed as the supreme value and is actively engaged in suppressing everything that claims to be higher than it. Moreover, it is necessary to take this into account to explain the situation of a Christian education or at least one imparted by Christians, which prides itself on teaching only what the non-Christian or anti-Christian schools teach and on teaching its own truth according to the spirit and methods of those who deny it.

A first glance at philosophical and religious education in American Christian schools in 1966, leaves a disconcerting and, to tell the truth, scarcely believable impression. Naturally, the defenders of the traditional order and of the doctrine recommend by the Church must be taken into account. Everywhere present, those defenders still risk being allowed to fall into oblivion. As there is more rejoicing in the press for one priest who abandons his state than for a thousand who persevere, a professor whose teaching is inspired by the principles of Thomas Aquinas, following the Church's directives, is guaranteed to pass unnoticed. He does not count. What he says no longer counts, or as they say, it *counts for nothing*. If he teaches that there is a God, it is useless to talk about it, because that is expected from him. If he undertakes to demonstrate it, nobody listens to him, because it is known in advance that in any case he would believe. But if he teaches that there is no God, it becomes interesting. It becomes exciting if the teacher is a priest or a laymen speaking in the name of a Christian thought aware of its deep requirements. One day in my presence, a well-known Christian philosopher said that speaking about God is too often a sign of atheism. It was the first meeting of the group that I attended; it was also the last, because if I cannot talk about God with a Christian, I do not find many topics of conversation.

I feel similar irritation when I see Catholics from every country and every kind of clerical garb (when they still have one) teach me to rethink my own religion anew, as they themselves understand it and no longer as the Church teaches it is. Invited to renew the bath water, they empty out the bathtub with the baby, and although they put a completely new one in its place, one hesitates to believe them when they assure that it is the same baby as the old one.

A common feature of the books teaching this new gospel presented according to the taste of the moment, is what Jacques Maritain calls their "chronolatry." The term deserves to be successful, because the mental vice it designates is at work everywhere and corrupts many disciplines where, in principle, time ought not to be made a concern. Under its form closest to philosophical discourse, chronolatry posits in principle that "everything changes," and two corollaries immediately follow: "what was true yesterday can no longer be true today," and "today is better than yesterday and less good than tomorrow." Personally, I hold that these three propositions are meaningless. Because, ultimately, "everything changes" is one of Heraclitus's propositions, and if everything has been changing for twenty-five centuries, it would be time that this change itself should cease to change. But the most interesting sophism that this proposition hides is the equation it postulates between the new and the better. Why is today's truth better than yesterday's, except because the permanent, immutable constraining necessity of the first laws of thought impose themselves in the mind of the new philosophers today as always and forever. The trascendentals do not change meaning when changing object. And without doubt, if change is what is real, change is being. If it is being, it is true. If it is true, it is good. And if it is a new good that replaces the old one, it is better. Since in their eyes that is the case, the chronolators are not to be reproached when they affirm that becoming has all the attributes of being. Except, since the attributes of change itself belong to it only in virtue of the immutable necessity of being, the latter cannot be denied without being confirmed.

Let us set aside the writings of obscure college professors longing for advancement, which they no doubt will achieve because no talent is required to make a scandal, and the small scandal they make will attract the favor of many teaching institutions to them. The only interesting chronolatry is that of the great doctrinaires who made it a philosophical dogma, sometimes even a religious dogma. In this order, *in principio erat Hegel*. The dialectical views of reality invoke him, whether they are dialectics of the spirit like his or dialectic of matter, like Marx's, Lenin's, Stalin's, and their tribe's, and finally Teilhard de Chardin's, whose gnosticism runs parallel to the Christian religion (I speak of his doctrine, not of his faith) without ever doing more than altering it. Today and for now, Hegel is our Aristotle. His language or some dialect issued from this common stock is what everyone speaks. So we cannot question Hegel without disqualifying ourselves, as formerly Aristotle could not be challenged before the masters and students of the university of Paris.

I cannot say to what point this situation leaves a Christian philosopher indifferent. From 1904 to 1907, when I studied at the Sorbonne, I never heard a single lecture on Hegel, and nobody ever spoke about him except Émile Boutroux, who one day, at the oral examination of a thesis I no longer recall, was amusing himself with the *concrete universal*, about which he said that Hegel never told us exactly what it was. I have the illusion of having understood it myself much later, but in my time Hegel "was never on the syllabus." Lucien Lévy-Bruhl preferred Comte's *Positive Philosophy* and Kant's *Pure Reason*; Victor Delbos preferred *Practical Reason*, Victor Brochard liked the Greeks (except Aristotle); and that accounts for almost everybody. That today Marx and Lenin bring back a Hegel turned upside down is a fact that presents real but contingent interest. It does not make necessary any updating of classical metaphysics from Parmenides to Plato. This is without philosophical importance unless someone attempts to impose that revision on us in the name of chronolatry. Hegel comes after Aristotle and Thomas Aquinas. That does not prove he was truer and *better*. Those who pretend this deny that there are absolutely true propositions in metaphysics precisely because it is wisdom about the unchangeable principles of the intellect. Thomism admits with Aristotle and Plato that the intelligible precedes the intellection in all true knowledge or, if we prefer, that the object precedes knowledge. That is what is called "realism." If there is a quarrel between Marxism and Christian philosophy, it has no impact up there. Both are realisms, one that identifies being with matter, the other that holds being equally transcends what, according to our experience, we call matter, spirit, and the existence of any being whatever. Marxism's materialism is what distinguishes us from it. Against this adversary, Thomas Aquinas would have patiently reworked the demonstration that two objects as differentiated by their properties as matter and thought could not be identical. With Hegel, on the contrary, according to whom the Idea and the Spirit are reality itself, no conversation is possible for a Christian aware of his faith's speculative implications. God transcends every being as an in-itself that owes nothing to the fact that I think it. To summon us to Hegelianize our theology under the pretext of rejuvenating it is an invitation to meaninglessness.

Jacques Maritain has no need of reinforcement, but he no longer tolerates tranquilizers. One day I asked him why he likes to place "*banderillas de fuego*" so often in the thick hides of his adversaries, which enrages them. "It is absolutely necessary," he said. I believe it would be necessary, if it were useful. Now, there was recently an opportunity to see that these *banderillas* leave the bull on whom they are stuck indifferent but exasperate people at whom they were not aimed. Certain of our best theologians are close to crying sacrilege if one permits himself to say that Hegel's philosophy is purely and simply false. "It comes back [to one of them] from different sources that excellent Catholic philosophers have been shocked by the expeditious manner in which Jacques Maritain dispatches Hegel or Husserl for that which he calls *ideosophy*." Analyzing the reason for the irritation at this summary liquidation, this theologian thinks they seem to be due to this: "The deviations that Jacques Maritain denounces stem from real problems and difficulties ... These problems are common to all those who work in the area of theology except for those, if there are any, who are not really informed."

The misunderstanding here that separates two (or three) friends stems from the term "theology," because neither Hegel nor Husserl nor the other ideosophs whom our criticism considers are Christian theologians. They are philosophers, authors of very interesting books upon which it is a pleasure to lecture, since their thought first of all refers to itself like that of any consistent idealism. Accordingly, there is no difference between understanding it and approving it. What a pleasure to teach Hegel! One cannot tire of admiring the industry with which this fabric of so admirably matched concept is woven. If by chance it further occurs to Hegel to say something that connects with the real, the wonderment is doubled because what he says is not only ingenious, it is true. What a problem our theologian poses for us, because a hundred times and more I have observed that philosophers give so much better lectures in the measure that they are more false! To make a good "course topic," a philosopher ought to have a system. Victor Brochard never taught Aristotle, because Aristotle has no system. Plato does not have one either, but Brochard loved him, so he manufactured a system for Plato. It is very necessary for professors to live by their teaching. Nobody intends to take the bread off their table by depriving them of discussing doctrines, true or false, that are a useful exercise for the mind. The Peasant of the Garonne[3] is not talking about that but about philosophy in its function and dignity as the "vassal of theology." When he liquidates all ideosophy that claims to exercise that function, he is unjust to no one, because Hegelianism is not the issue, but it is true that every idealism is a plague and poison for Christian theology into which someone desires to introduce that idealism. The object of Christian theology is a transcendent datum that thought cannot claim to draw out of itself without annihilating it.

The root of the misunderstanding can only be uncovered further on. Our theologian talks about *The Peasant of the Garonne* as if the book's object were to put together a panorama of the Council's work and do justice to those whose labor prepared it. "Where does pastoral renovation appear in this book?", the critic asks, "Where are the dogmatic works of Karl Rahner or Schillebeeck? Where does the immense Biblical activity of recent decades appear? Isn't that theology?" Yes, indisputably, and who could ignore it? But our theologian, completely absorbed by what the Council has done, does not seem clearly aware of what the Council has not done. "For me," good Pope John said to me one day, "theology is *Our Father who art in heaven.*" Without claiming to guess about the testimony of history that will not be written for a long time, I suggest that the Council, which was John

---

3   [Translator, the peasant is Jacques Maritain author of *Le Paysan de la Garonne, Un vieux laïc s'interroge à propos du temps présent*, Paris: Desclée de Brouwer, 1967. *The Peasant of the Garonne: An Old Layman Questions Himself about the Present Time*, translated by Michael Cuddihy and Elizabeth Hughes, New York: Holt, Rinehart & Winston, 1968.]

XXIII's Council first, remained faithful to his spirit to the end. If it were not unbecoming to judge in such a matter, I would say that this heroic fidelity to the undertaking's original design was supreme wisdom on Pope Paul VI's part. It is true that pastoral, liturgical, ecclesiological, and Biblical theology were well represented there, but the theology of which Jacques Maritain does not speak but that he embodies throughout a whole life's work, never really got a hearing there. Scholastic theology, neglected today when it is not scorned, rather shone by its absence. The consequences were felt during the Council. Extravagant positions were held by certain pastors about whom one wondered where they led their flocks. The Synagogue would have expelled them in order to stone them on the spot. Nowadays, these consequences unfold with disturbing regularity because all Biblical, pastoral, or other theology ultimately leads to dogmatic expressions, and whether we seek commentary in the Church Fathers (patristic theology) or in medieval theologians (Scholastic theology), we always find ourselves led to some language of philosophical origin. The teaching of dogmatic theology is linked, in fact and by necessity, to the categories and language of certain philosophers. That link begins with St. Paul and the fourth gospel. The first disorder always seeps into that linkage, which is what the Peasant of the Garonne is rightly uneasy about.

Jacques Maritain's book is not a picture or balance of the Council. It is a post-conciliar memoir. It is an appeal for vigilance, alerting us in the face of the wreckage piling up on the moral and pastoral level, because dogmatic truth has been partly lost from sight. Listening to some sermons today, one thinks that perhaps Christianity ought to follow its faithful, rather than some of its priests. We hope to be able to be excused from recalling that St. Thomas "is not the only valid human source of true philosophical and theological knowledge." Who was ever so simple as to think so and so indifferent to ridicule to say so? How might I make our theologian's friends perceive that a book like *The Peasant of the Garonne* is not a balance of the council nor a theological summa but a cry of distress in the face of post-conciliar ruins that pile up around us, an answer to those complaints, and those tears (yes, I have seen them) of priests who do not know to whom they can confide their dismay. For we do not ask that philosophical and theological Thomism be imposed, without which one can certainly be saved, but we would like the creeds, which express salvific truth, to not be destroyed. If nobody knows their real meaning any more, no one will remain to understand and confess them. They already want to make us confess others. This disaster will not be avoided without a doctrinal rule, acknowledged as such, which those who profess one same faith accept as the rule.

The Council was the work of truly supernatural courage. For more than three centuries the Church was harshly blamed for not having taken the initiative to make necessary reforms in the sixteenth century. Regret has often been expressed that Martin Luther left the Church instead of staying to reform it from within. This time the lesson was learned, because many small-time reformers actively devote themselves to changing received traditions often from one year to another, without anything being done to brake their reforming passion. Doubtless, all this was inevitable, but the actual result of putting sixteen conciliar documents into effect has the consequence of overturning customs in a manner all the more disconcerting to the faithful in that diocesan or parochial reformers do not always agree among themselves. A little while ago, nothing resembled one Mass more than another Mass. Without even talking about the rock Masses accompanied by guitars and embellished by longhaired deaconesses in charge of reading the gospel, it must be recognized that two public Masses are rarely celebrated identically today. There is one single concern common to all the individual reforms: to occupy the public in some way, while the priest for his part says a Mass with no great relation to what the faithful say or chant. Some of the most beautiful parts of the liturgy fall into oblivion little by little. *Deus qui humanae substantiae dignitatem mirabiliter condidisti et mirabilius reformasti*—who still knows this sublime prayer? It is true the churches are empty and the number of priests diminishes at an alarming rate, but what is being done is not done to reverse the tendency. Perhaps these are not the necessary reforms to which the Council summoned us.

The most troubling thing is something else. The priest who reduces the teaching and practice of his religion to its simplest terms in order to facilitate an unsophisticated public's access to it, knows very well that each of his gestures, each of his words, go infinitely beyond what these faithful understand about them, but this does not seem to be the question. Religious life and practices are not the business of science but of faith and piety. Liturgy and catechism have the goal of assuring contact between the belief and the spiritual reality that is the object of his religion. The apostle's creed says what the Christian believes about God. Conciliar decisions and authoritative theological commentaries do no more than define and specify the meaning of those articles of faith. As expressions reflecting the Church's belief, these formulas are sacred and the truths they express are immutable like God himself. All have difficulties, all challenge mere reason, and all demand from human nature an effort of submission and even sacrifice. But St. Paul said that once and for all, speaking of the madness and scandal in relation to the mystery of the cross. If we abandon the believer's reason and thought to their natural inclination, their spontaneous impulse will be to reduce everything to terms that cannot be suspected of scandal and madness. Left to the natural preference of its author, every reform of this sort spontaneously will tend to "naturalize" faith and its objects. This is why Christian dogmas come back to us today demythified or even, as they say, demystified. A naturalized religion will in fact have no other mysteries but those of nature. They are enough, it is thought, to keep reason at bay without the need to add anything. But mysteries of faith are different from those of nature in that they have God as their object, so much so that to naturalize their object amounts to suppressing it. Certain of our theologians leave us in difficulty on this particular point, because then the problem is posed far beyond the material details of rite or the level of the reality signified by the rite, that of *res* not *signum*. Real dismay seizes the faithful then, because they no longer know what they ought to believe and because when they consult theologians, they end up doubting that the theologians themselves know. When the unity of faith ceases, Christianity also ceases,

This is the only reason that makes Teilhard de Chardin case be of any interest. His person and his faith are not at issue. No question is posed about him as long as someone does not want to make us admit that his thought is indeed the Church's, because then we are put in the situation of choosing between the Church and him. It is true that theological updating can require us to adhere to new theological propositions or simply to ones whose formulation differ from those to which we mistakenly imagined that the Church's teaching was linked. That may be, but if it is so, it is for our theologians to tell us. Their responses to our questions lack clarity in this regard.

Was Teilhard a great scientist or not? Perhaps the question has no meaning, and in any case, it has no religious meaning. Let us leave science to the scientist. Teilhard certainly was not a scholastic theologian. He was not a great or minor scholastic theologian; he was not one in any sense. Neither was he a theologian of the patristic type, because his theological activity was a reflection on science, not on Holy Scripture. It may perhaps be a religious interpretation of *The Origin of Species*; it is not a reflection on *In Hexameron* in the spirit of St. Basil and St. Augustine. There, it seems, is the heart of the problem. Teilhard might have had a philosophical theology like Plato's, which I do not believe, or a scientific theology like Aristotle's, which I rather tend to think, except that in his case Heraclitus and his spiritual family replace peripatetic fixism by mobilism. However, if all Christian theology deals first and necessarily with the supernatural revelation of the word of God in Scripture, it seems rather difficult for Teilhardism to be Christian theology. It matters little that he should know and quote Scripture or not, nor that it should have nourished or not nourished his piety. The question is only to know whether Teilhard's thought re-encounters the Church's thought by whatever path it may have proceeded to re-encounter it.

It is rather easy to explain the insistence of some Christians, unpleasant for themselves, who do not speak as theologians but as simple faithful, who underline the gap between Teilhard's theology and the Church's. It is a matter of intelligent understanding and of reason. If Teilhard's teaching is that of the Church, they no longer know what to believe, because they do not recognize the object of their faith. That Teilhard could not believe in what is called original sin is possible, and he is not the only one to feel perplexed before this mystery. One simply asks whether the Church is ready to dispense the faithful from believing in it. The doctrine is so constant and central; it is so linked to St. Paul's teaching and to the very dogma of the redemption, that Catholics brought up in the pre-Teilhardian faith make no difference between the concepts of *Christ* and of *Redeemer*. If this knot yields, the entire fabric comes undone. What perplexes us, what disturbs us sometimes to the point of irritation, is not that Teilhard might not believe in original sin. That is his business. Nor is it that others follow him on this point. That is their responsibility. It is not even that certain theologians might approve it. It is only that approving it or not, someone should want to make us believe that a theology without sin is Christian theology. For, *Christian* implies *Christ*, and what did the lamb who takes away the sins of the world come to do, if the world is without sin? We are not dealing with a detail here, but with the very substance of the Christian faith. The Molinists did not agree with the Thomists on the modalities of humanity's justification by Christ, but it did not enter their mind that humanity had not been justified.

This confirms that the Teilhardian state of humanity is that of natural innocence, lack of awareness of sin. His optimism has often been noted and indeed it is difficult to deny his confidence in matter, not only as it is in itself, which responds to its Creator's own testimony when he looked at his work and saw that it was good, but as it has become after the fall. More-over, it is probable that this intellectual, who was only interested in ideas and knowledge, may have been spared the travails of the flesh: St. Thomas himself said that the exercise of the intelligence was the most effective de-fense against temptation. However that may be, Teilhard does not place great value on chastity. Few aspects of his thought are as interesting as study-ing what he admired in women after reaching the age of thirty, which saw a late awakening of the sense of the eternal feminine in him. Far from seeing a fall of Teilhard into sensuality there, as some do, I would instead see the indication of such perfect purity of heart that he was unaware of the dangers of the senses or was led to minimize them by lacking a perception of its risk in himself. He certainly was not unaware of temptations, because he said that faced with them the only effective prudent thing was to burn with a stronger fire. Neither did he condemn asceticism, nor deny the prudence of flight before the occasion of sin. He only observed that, "The moral value (or at least the significance) and traditional discipline of chastity are in the process of losing their evidence for many among us," but in that he sees less the sign of regression than an "attraction toward a new ideal."

An attraction is always the work of an omega. Why think badly of mat-ter, since it is the matrix of the Spirit. The idea that there exists a universal genesis of the spirit through matter (the idea, in other words of a *spiritual power of Matter*) submerges the problem of chastity in its origins. And there we are again. Evolution, the idea that haunts Teilhard de Chardin, seizes his thought once again. As always, it is an evolution from below to above, from matter to spirit, because "the evolution of our ideas about matter" has ended by revealing all its possibilities to us, or at least their unexpected ex-tension. What troubles him in the cult to chastity is certainly the contempt for matter that it implies. A strange lyrical dread grips him at the thought that the *perfect* might almost have blocked the progress of matter's evolution and the "conception of spirit, still in progress." This danger seems to him to be happily warded off. The transformation of our conception of matter has been extended to the realm of our sentimental life: "Woman is for man the symbol of all the universe's hoped for complementarities... At the end of the spiritual power of Matter, the spiritual power of the flesh and of the feminine."

It is not possible to follow Fr. Teilhard in the exegesis where his reverie leads him. Let us rather take his clear, simple opinions, whose sense no exegete can annul: "We already said it above. The material side of virginity, important for primitive people, has completely stopped interesting us. The virtue's physical aspect has become unintelligible for us." It is easy to see that a male is speaking, but I have nothing to object to that. If he believes these things, why should he not say them? He himself foresees that he will be accused of naiveté for counseling a kind of transchastity where souls could be united beyond bodies, but that is not the question here. The issue is to know whether this complete scorn for virginity in its exact literal sense, is in agreement with Christian tradition. Teilhard de Chardin cannot be touched without religious, prelates, and theologians of every stripe raising their voices and pens to justify him. They have an easy task, because this *philanderous* thought evades analysis. He is easily justified for having said one thing by proving he has also said the opposite, and it is useless to want to be precise, because we never will know which of two contraries ought to be attributed to his account. Worse yet, it is never completely sure that those who defend him do not think like him at bottom, because when questions are posed, they do not excuse their great man, they accuse those who ask about him. When the accused is a layman and the accuser a priest, the accused no longer knows. He wonders who is right. Since the issue is theology and Christian faith, evidently the priest is right. But, if what the priest says is not believable for the layman, he becomes troubled. Is he the victim of prejudices that the Church herself asks him to reject? Or is the priest in the vanguard of that craze for novelty that blinds him to the true meaning of the message he has the mission of transmitting? If there is an arbiter, where is he?

Whatever the answer is, the evil is there, and it most pathetic victims are the forty-year-old priests who wonder where the truth is that they have sworn to serve. Where is the Church to which their youth was one day consecrated?

I see just one answer to that. The only effective memory to the malaise is to assign again a place of honor to the traditional theology that Pope Paul VI has urged us to respect, follow, and advocate. I will not repeat here which theology. The popes have said it. I have repeated it after them, not only on their word alone but constrained, as it were, by the testimony of the truth. If I am mistaken, that is a disorder. If so many guides in Europe and America lose their way bringing others who have lost their way in their wake, the disorder is still worse. But the most troubling thing of all is not knowing who is mistaken, oneself or the others, and bearing within oneself the fear of being unwittingly one of the causes of the disorder that is being denounced. Does not deploring the ruins in the midst of which we find ourselves increase the number of ruins? In this uncertainty, I see no other hope than a return to the Wisdom of the schools, daughter and handmaiden of the faith, mistress of the true, and intelligent judge of necessary discernment, because if it were admitted that pastoral theology could do without dogmatic theology with impunity, the worst would not be something to anticipate, it would have already happened.

Postscript

Writing these pages, I have asked myself several times whether I was giving in to the pessimism of old age or at least whether I was not letting myself be unduly influenced by some incidents without lasting effect. Above all, I wondered whether the crisis I was talking about was real or the creature of my imagination.

The answer to these questions came when the book was already printed. It is irrefutable, and I can do no more than reproduce it as it stands, because one does not comment upon an apostolic letter. The Pope is infallible in these matters; no commentator is. It is for the commentator to check himself in the light of the Pope's word.

Since the Catholic press gave this document minimal publicity, and I only knew of its existence through the journal *Itinéraires*, I specify that I take the text from the pamphlet *Petrum et Paulum*, apostolic letter of his Holiness Pope Paul VI, Éditions du Cèdre, 13, rue Mazarine, Paris, 1967. The apostolic brief is dated February 22, 1967, the feast of the Chair of St. Peter. Here I only cite the passage from the document relative to the crisis of the so-called *post-conciliar* period, about which our little book tries to speak. The French text published by Éditions du Cèdre follows that of the *Osservatore Romano*. Here is the passage in question:

> Since the religious sense, by which faith is supported as upon its natural foundation, is diminished among the people of our time, here and there in the field of Catholic doctrine, new exegetical or theological opinions are often taken from philosophers, bold but inept in their doctrine.
>
> These opinions not only call into doubt the genuine meaning of the truths the Church teaches with authority, but the norm of Church magisterium is neglected under the guise of adapting

religious truth to the mentality of our time, the pursuit of theological investigation is utterly shaped by the whims of what is called *historicism*, some dare to deny the sacred character and trustworthiness of the testimony of Holy Scripture, the historical and sacred character of the testimony of Holy Scripture, and the attempt is made to introduce a so-called *post-conciliar mentality* among the people of God.

Now, that mentality that neglects the strong cohesion that articulates the Ecumenical Council's abundant and magnificent output of doctrine and law with the sacred patrimony of Church magisterium and discipline, thus seeking to destroy the traditional care for fidelity to the Church and to propagate a vain hope by giving a new interpretation of the Christian religion, which, however, could only be unfounded and sterile. What would remain of the truths of faith or of the theological virtue by which we believe them, if such attempts, withdrawn from the authority of Church magisterium, should come to be successful?[1]

Perhaps I am mistaken, but it seems impossible to me to be clearer and to multiply exhortation more generously to avoid condemnation. Taking advantage of the nineteenth centenary of the martyrdom of the two apostles Peter and Paul, one the Church's foundation, the other Teacher of Nations, the Pope announces that the whole year from June 29, 1967 to June 29, 1968 will bear the title "Year of Faith," that the chant and recitation of the *Credo* will have the place of honor in it. Finally, summing up the whole

---

1   [translator: The Vatican website www.vatican.va/holy_father/paul_vi /apost_exhortations /documents/ hf_p-vi_exh_19670222_petrum-et-paulum_It.html describes the document as an Apostolic Exhortation. It is available in Latin and Italian. I have used the Latin as a check on the French version that Gilson cites. The ellipsis in the second quotation is for sources omitted. For a published edition in English, Pope Paul VI, Apostolic Exhortation on the Nineteenth Centenary of the Martyrdom of *SS. Peter and Paul. Petrum et Paulum Apostolos*, January 1, 1967, United States Catholic Conference.]

message in a single phrase, each segment of which is inseparable from the rest, the Pope sees an invitation in this anniversary to prolong the effort of Vatican II, itself the coronation of Vatican I, which has not come, we ourselves say, *solvere sed adimplere*:

> Now indeed to fortify our faith expressed in its correct meaning, to stimulate the study of the teachings that have been recently set forth by the Ecumenical Council, to sustain the efforts of Catholics who seek new ways of expounding the truths of faith but fully agreeing with the deposit of Church teaching, with the same meaning and the same way of thinking (*eodem sensu eademque sententia*, Vincent of Lerins ...), we say, after a certain space of time has passed, to achieve all these things, happily the solemn centenaries of the Apostles are approaching. They offer all the children of the Church a dual opportunity: in the first place that they may respond with these words full of humility and grandeur *I believe* to Jesus Christ, Son of God, Mediator and Consummator of our Faith, that is, namely, that they may give the full assent of intellect and will to his word and to his announcement of his Person and his salvation, ... so that they may follow those greatest witness to Christ with due honor, renewing the Christian resolve of sincerely and actively profession our faith and theirs and also toiling in prayer and deed for the unity of the same faith to be restored among all Christians.

To this, one can add only one word: Amen.

Paris, May 26, 1967.

Index of Names